It Ain't Rocket Science:

College Counseling for Everyone

By Akhee Jamiel Williams

Additional Titles by the Author:

The Truth Between the Lines: From History to Our Story, and

Beyond

Divided We Fall. Ignorant We Fail.

To Maxwell and Malcolm

Table of Contents

A Note to the Reader

Dear Students, Parents, Colleagues, Educators and Counselors,

Allow me to introduce myself. My name is Akhee Jamiel Williams, but you can call me A.J., for short. I am an Admission Counselor, meaning I am one of those people who decide whether or not you, or your student, or students in general, get into college. And yes, it's Admission, not *"Admissions,"* although I wouldn't correct you if you said it that way because I'm not that pretentious. It's the old "tuh-may-toh vs. ta-mah-toh" debate in action; and it's tomato, by the way. The bottom line is people use the two interchangeably, and it's not that big of a deal either way. It's a free country, say it however you like. Semantic diatribes aside, I am one of *those people*. A decision-maker, a guardian of the Ivory Tower, a gatekeeper, if you will. And I've been at it for a while now: over fifteen years at this point.

My daily duties include being the first point of contact for most of the prospective students and families that I meet, either out on the road visiting high schools, at college fairs, or on campus during their visit. Myself, and my colleagues in the profession, are essentially the sales force for our respective institutions. Although I think it's safe to say that most of us pride ourselves on the fact that we do more educating than selling; a point driven home by the fact that we are paid like educators and not salespeople. There are no bonuses for apps read or students enrolled. Not on the non-profit side, at least. Nor should there be. We represent a single option in a vast sea of options, and no one option is the best fit for every student. Most of us get that; at least those of us who care do.

Other duties include reading applications, many thousands of applications. I work in Undergraduate Admission, so that means I focus on the applications of first-year, or *freshmen* (Hint: you should be using "first-year" now) applicants, as well as transfer applicants. I probably average around 2,000 applications a year, which puts my total at upwards of 30,000 applications read over my career. Additional job responsibilities entail working with counselors at the high school level, professors and administrators on campus -from the President on down- engaging in exciting and fun conversations when decisions go out, and dealing with difficult discussions when the decision or financial aid package isn't quite what someone wanted or expected.

The travel component is fun. At least it can be for the first few years and the first few weeks of a given travel season. My colleagues and I crisscross the country, and some of us the globe, all to spread the good word about our respective institutions, and really higher education in general. We visit junior high and high schools, elementary schools (sometimes) and non-profit organizations, churches and community colleges. You name the type of institution, we've probably visited it. We go everywhere: the inner cities, the suburbs, the ex-burbs (that's a thing now, I guess), the country-side, anywhere there are students to be reached.

And all of that is enjoyable, for sure. Or at least it can be, just as much as it can become tedious and monotonous, like any repetitive task. But the one responsibility that I really like, the one that has probably kept me in the profession above all else, is the Information Session. That is the part of the job that I truly enjoy most. It's what keeps me engaged and motivated in what I do. That's when the bright lights come on, the stage is set, and *it's showtime,* so to speak. For those of you who don't know what an information session is, it is essentially the opportunity for the Admission Counselor to inform you, the prospective student, parent, or counselor, about all that our wonderful institution has to offer. It's where we describe the various qualities of our campus and academic offerings, extoll the virtues of our facilities, tell you how many PhD's we have teaching, all the opportunities you'll have to do research as an undergraduate, the places you'll get to travel through study abroad, and how we're so cool and all other schools drool, etc. It's where the application and admission process is explained. Where costs are discussed and financial aid options are laid out. It's all of that and then some. And for most, that's all it is.

I see it, however, as an opportunity for more. I see it as the small window that I have to actually *inform* you. About my institution of course, obviously, because it's awesome, and they pay me! But I like to inform folks about all institutions, or at least distinguish between the different types of institutions that they have to choose from; and in so doing, give them context with regards to the type of institution I represent. I like to talk to them about the benefits of being educated, and therefore inspire them to *actively* pursue their education, be it at my university or not. For those brief few minutes I have with an audience, I attempt to shed as much light on the college search journey as I possibly can; to demystify this whole college admission process. And I'm good at it. Like, really good at it. (*The not-so-humble brag*) I know my stuff.

Whether it be a classroom of disadvantaged at-risk teens, a presentation space filled with middle-class and well-to-do families, or a conference ballroom with folks from all walks of life in attendance, I know they're paying attention when their eyes are locked-in with mine. When they're quiet, but actively listening. I love it when heads nod, when jokes land, when parents laugh too loudly and students shake their heads in embarrassment, when subtle information is picked up by the mom in the third row, or by the knucklehead student in the back that has all of a sudden shaped-up and stopped talking. I know when I've got them, and when we're all in for this ride together. I love that feeling. I enjoy that shared experience.

That is why I decided to compose this treatise; this *white paper* on College Admission. It dawned on me that those interactions were merely a drop in the bucket, in the grand scheme of things. Sure, I've *hopefully* made an impact with the people I've encountered throughout the years. But what about all those other students I'm not able to get in front of? What about those families that can't make the trip to my campus? What about all those counselors and educators who could really use the reinforcement of this message for their students, who I'm simply not able to reach? Well, this book is my answer to that.

So let's start with what this book is not. It is not a tell-all. It is not an exposé intended to spill industry secrets or air out dirty laundry. Because even in The World of Admission *snitches get stitches!* It is not a "College Admission For Dummies" book. And it most certainly does not contain the secret formula to Ivy League acceptance, or acceptance to any particular campus, for that matter. What it is, is an extension of my vocation. It's my version of social justice in action; of servicing a need I see in society and attempting to reach as many individuals as I can with this message. It is missionary work, if you will, my spreading of the Good Word: the Gospel of Education, and its healing powers. And that, folks, is enough about me.

Intro

Let's get things started with one clear and guiding principle: Education is important. Education is good. Education is key to opportunities and socioeconomic advancement. More tangible than power, per se, education is elevation − out of ignorance, out of poverty, out of oppression. And therein lies its true power.

Study after study shows that the more educated an individual is the higher their earnings over a lifetime, the higher their job satisfaction and chances of receiving benefits like life insurance and healthcare, the healthier their lifestyles, and the lower their chances of living in poverty or reliant upon public assistance. [1] In general, the more educated an individual is, on average, the better their quality of life.

But it's a slow burn. An education takes years to attain and potentially thousands of dollars to achieve. So even in the pursuit of an education one must be smart about their approach. Everyone has heard the Siren's tales of individuals accumulating insurmountable debt in their pursuit of an education. Suffice it to say that those individuals, in the most extreme cases at least, went about it the wrong way. There is a better and smarter approach to attaining an education. Debt is a reality of educational attainment, and it always will be. But the smart folks –the realistic folks– take on a manageable amount of it.

That *smart approach* to achieving an education is what this book is about. It's about realizing the benefits of being educated, and cultivating one's options in attaining it. It's about demystifying the pursuit of higher education, and explaining that this is not, in fact, rocket science. There are literally thousands of college options in this country and beyond. There is only so much that college Admission professionals, like myself, can take into consideration when making decisions. And students, parents, and counselors alike must simply follow the guidelines which have been laid before them, and which we will discuss in detail in this book.

Let's begin, shall we.

Chapter 1:

The Benefits of Being Educated

If we are to have this conversation about educational attainment, or any conversation of substance truly worth having, I always find it best when we begin with some common ground, or at least a basic understanding of the realities at hand. And when discussing the importance of being educated there is probably no more impactful place to start than a discussion of demographics and socioeconomics; because numbers don't lie.

According to the United States Census Bureau Current Population Survey, the estimated population for the continental U.S. as of January 1, 2019, was 328,467,812. [2] However, depending on how you search or what you search for on the Census Bureau website, you may come up with different answers. The American Community Survey, for example, another study produced by the U.S. Census Bureau, annually reports five-year estimate data. For the years 2013-17 the ACS reported that the estimated U.S. population was a little over 321,000,000. [3] Thus, for our purposes, and for the sake of argument, or consistency at least, our conversation will utilize the more conservative five-year estimate of 321 million.

The racial and ethnic breakdown of the population, according to that figure, is that the country is about 64% white, 16% Hispanic / Latino, 13% black or African-American, about 6% Asian, and 1% Native American, Alaskan, and Hawaiian combined. Mixed-race individuals account for about 3% of the U.S. population. [4]

Why does that matter? Well for the purposes of this conversation, those numbers will help in framing some of the realities of educational attainment, representation at the high school level and on college campuses, poverty rates as a whole and the amount of individuals in certain groups in poverty, etc. But more importantly, those numbers can help to shed light on just how important an education can be for any one individual from any one of the many racial and ethnic groups that make up this great country; of how much of a game changer, potentially, a college education can be. And while there are certainly many historical, political, cultural, economic, criminal justice, social justice, and media related issues at play for the realities of all of those groups, we will, as best as possible, attempt to steer clear of those conversations; in this book, at least. I've written extensively on those topics, and will continue to do so, I'm sure. But this conversation is about education, and simply highlighting its importance; regardless of race, creed, color, or background.

In good news, high school completion is currently the highest it has ever been in America. A December 2017 press release from the U.S. Census Bureau praised data that indicated ninety percent of the population age twenty-five and older had completed high school. [5] And educational attainment in general is on the rise as 55.4% of the same age range had completed high school and some college, with thirty-four percent having completed a bachelor's degree or higher. [6] According to the 2017 ACS (for year's 2013-17) [7]:

- 92% of Whites were HS graduates or higher; 34.5% had a Bachelor's degree or higher
- 86.5% of Asians were HS graduates or higher; a whopping 53% had a B.A. or higher
- 85% of Blacks or African-Americans were HS grads or higher; 20.6% had a B.A. or higher
- 67% of Hispanic / Latinos were HS grads or higher; 15% had a B.A. or higher

The Non-Hispanic White group comprises 157,736,000 or **sixty-four percent** [8] of the 18 years and over U.S. population. For that group, 22.6% has attained a Bachelor's degree, and a combined thirteen percent have attained a Master's degree or higher.

At nearly 119 million more individuals than the next largest ethnic group in this age range alone, it is clear that the White or Caucasian demographic is the largest ethnic group in the country. America is, was, and will for the foreseeable future be, a white majority country, regardless of what population forecasts say. And by that, I mean that they will always be the largest ethnic group in the country. Even the most dire population forecasts predicting birth-dearths and ethnic-makeup shifts still put Caucasians at fifty percent of the U.S. population many years down the line. Which is, in many respects, a sizeable shift from sixty-five percent, but it's not the earth-shattering, end of days, apocalyptic tale of white atrophy that folks can sometimes make it out to be. The point being, there are *a lot* of white folks out there. The term "minority" isn't just a descriptor for *others*, it is a statistical reality; a point I always attempt to explain to folks who ask about diversity on college campuses or the lack thereof. Campuses, especially college campuses, are merely microcosms of the neighborhood, city, region, or country in which they are located.

Speaking of location, I find it interesting, and useful for such discussions, to have a sense of where the concentration of specific ethnic or racial groups are throughout the country. This helps one to understand why he or she sees more or less of individuals that look like them in a particular region, state, city, neighborhood, high school or college campus, for example. And for the white or Caucasian demographic the best description of where they are is *everywhere*: literally.

CensusScope.org is a product of the Social Science Data Analysis Network [9], which is an offshoot of the University of Michigan's Institute for Social Research. They produce some very interesting demographic data, some of which are color-coded maps displaying the concentration of various ethnic and racial groups. Based on the year 2000 Census Data, they produced the following map which delineates counties throughout the country for which the Non-Hispanic white population was either above or below eighty percent; as in comprising 8 out of 10 people in a given county. [10]

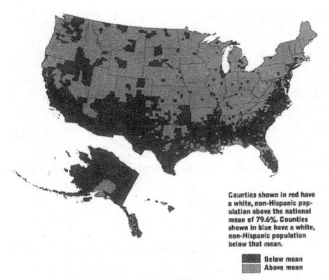

Counties shown in red have
a white, non-Hispanic population above the national
mean of 79.6%. Counties
shown in blue have a white,
non-Hispanic population
below that mean.

■ Below mean
□ Above mean

Non-Hispanic whites account for 69.1 percent of the U.S. population, according to the 2000 Census data.
However, because the non-white population is heavily clustered in relatively few counties, the median U.S.
county has a population that is 79.6% non-Hispanic white.

Source: Census 2000 analyzed by the Social Science Data Analysis Network (SSDAN).

As there have been no *major* ethnic or racial migrations within the country for the past several years, aside from a steady but declining influx of Hispanic immigrants in the West and Southwest, it's pretty safe to assume that, demographically speaking, things look about the same today as they did in 2000.

So, back to our main point of discussion, what does all this mean for the Caucasian population in terms of educational attainment? Well, while only twenty-two percent of the 18 and over segment has attained at least a Bachelor's degree, at 34.7 million individuals that is almost 4 million more *white college graduates* than there are African-Americans in the 18 and over age range, period. Fifteen million whites have attained a Master's degree and 5.4 million have achieved a Professional or Doctoral degree. [11]

The next largest ethnic group, Hispanic / Latinos, who account for well over 50 million Americans, comprise some 39,170,000 or **sixteen percent** of the 18 years and over U.S. population. For that group only eleven percent has attained a Bachelor's degree, and a combined 4.2% (1.6 million) have attained a Master's degree or higher. In terms of where this Hispanic / Latino demographic -predominantly comprised of Mexican, Puerto Rican and Cuban heritage, amongst several other Central and South American ethnicities- is concentrated, the majority reside in the West and Southwestern regions of the country, with pockets of concentration in Florida and along the Eastern Coast; primarily in major cities. [12]

The African-American or Black group comprises 30,847,000 or **12.5%** of the 18 years and over U.S. population. For that group, fourteen percent has attained a Bachelor's degree, and a combined 7.6% (2.3 million) have attained a Master's degree or higher. The African-American demographic is overwhelmingly concentrated in the South, with about fifty percent of the population residing there. The East Coast and Mid-west have nearly an equal share, and less than ten percent of the African-American population resides on the West Coast. Aside from the South, African-Americans are primarily centered in and around major cities. [13]

The Asian-American group, which itself is comprised of over 40 different ethnic groups, with varying degrees of attachment to education, accounts for 15,005,000 or about **six percent** of the 18 years and over U.S. population. For that group, 28.6% has attained a Bachelor's degree, and a combined twenty-two percent have attained a Master's degree or higher; the highest percentage by far of any ethnic group. In fact, while accounting for nearly 24 million less individuals in the 18 years and older age range, the Asian population has about 400,000 more Doctorates than the largest minority population, the Hispanic-Latino demographic. The Asian population is primarily found on either coast, with California being home to the largest percentage of the group. [14]

While the Hispanic / Latino demographic receives far more attention in news and media coverage for population growth and immigration, the Asian-American population has, for some years now, been the fastest growing minority group in the United States [15]. That growth, however, comes from a much smaller base to begin with as Asians only account for about six percent of the population. Indian Americans, along with Chinese, Korean, and Japanese Americans, in particular, demonstrate an unparalleled dedication to educational attainment, and are a driving force behind the reality that the group's post-secondary degree attainment is so much higher, percentage-wise, than any other group. And while Vietnamese, Thai, Laotian, and Pakistani families demonstrate a similar academic devotion, as ethnic groups their economic realities have played out somewhat differently. That said, the Asian-American contingent, as a whole, is a socioeconomic powerhouse. They came. They learned the rules of the game. And they have advanced accordingly.

So why is educational attainment an important metric to track? It all stems from a time-tested, scientifically proven formula that I developed several years ago and have been sharing with groups far and wide for years now. An edict sure to be revered and repeated in the educational lexicon for generations to come. An *Academic Law*, if you will, akin to Newton's Laws in the scientific community. An equation which reads as follows:

$$Education + Time = \$\$$$

Boom! That just happened! Education plus time equals dollar signs. Truly mind-blowing stuff, right?!.... And of course, the answer to that is no, that is not paradigm-shifting, mind-blowing stuff. It's not even all that inventive, if you think about it. But it is short. And it does rhyme. All of which helps one to remember it over time. That equation, *Education + Time = $$*, is about as straightforward and basic a concept as it gets. Once again, all together now, let's repeat our mantra, "It ain't rocket science!" That formula represents a simple reality which is easily illustrated when you look at the demographics and socioeconomics of the country: the more educated an individual, the more likely that individual is to be compensated as such. There is a reason that the national average for minimum wage is $7.25 an hour [16], and Anesthesiologists earn three to $400,000 annually. The level of training and expertise required in anesthetizing and reviving surgical patients is exponentially higher than that for the person working the fry station. Thus, the jobs are rewarded accordingly.

To be clear, what that equation does not state is that one is guaranteed to be more successful than another simply because he or she is more educated. It simply states that one's chances to improve his or her earning potential, and potential for employment in general, are greatly increased the higher their level of education. As demonstrated below:

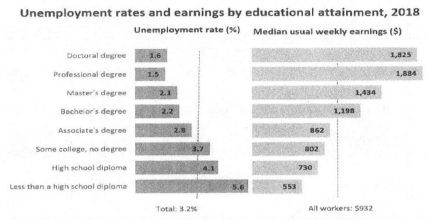

Unemployment rates and earnings by educational attainment, 2018

Unemployment rate (%)   Median usual weekly earnings ($)

Education level	Unemployment rate (%)	Median weekly earnings ($)
Doctoral degree	1.6	1,825
Professional degree	1.5	1,884
Master's degree	2.1	1,434
Bachelor's degree	2.2	1,198
Associate's degree	2.8	862
Some college, no degree	3.7	802
High school diploma	4.1	730
Less than a high school diploma	5.6	553

Total: 3.2%   All workers: $932

Note: Data are for persons age 25 and over. Earnings are for full-time wage and salary workers.
Source: U.S. Bureau of Labor Statistics, Current Population Survey.

[17]

As the 2017 American Community Survey [18] demonstrates, for individuals 25 years of age and older, working full-time, the median earnings over a 12 month span were:

All	$37,913
Less than high school graduate	$21,738
High School graduate	$29,815
Some college or Associate's degree	$35,394

Bachelor's degree $52,019

Graduate or professional degree $69,903

A 2017 report from the U.S. Department of Commerce stated that the official poverty rate for that year was 12.3%, which equated to 39.7 million Americans. [19] Meaning nearly 40 million Americans lived in conditions that the United States government would characterize as sub-standard for the average American. Additionally, those with at least a Bachelor's degree had the lowest poverty rate. [20] In line with that, the previously mentioned 2017 American Community Survey reported the poverty rate for individuals 25 years or older, correlated to educational attainment, as follows: [21]

Less than high school graduate   26.4%

High school graduates   14%

Some college or Associate's degree   10.2%

Bachelor's degree or higher   4.5%

I'm no economist, but those are some pretty clear trends to me. The more educated an individual, the more they tend to earn. The more educated an individual, the less likely they are to live in poverty. Those points alone are two very strong arguments for the benefit of being educated; aside from an increased breadth of knowledge in general, and a presumably more informed worldview.

A pause for Clarity:

The Achievement Gap

The Achievement Gap, as defined by the good folks at The Glossary of Education Reform [22], "refers to any significant and persistent disparity in academic performance or educational attainment between different groups of students, such as whites and minorities, for example, or students from higher-income and lower-income households." [23]

Persistent being the key word here. This is no "one-off" occurrence, per say. This is a sustained difference in outcomes for certain groups, academically speaking, over a prolonged period of time. As a seasoned college Admission professional, I am here to tell you the Achievement Gap is real. I see it on a daily basis. And by no stretch of the imagination does it mean that one group in particular, or certain groups as a whole, are naturally smarter or more proficient, academically, than others. It's simply the reality of a system designed to produce such a result; as we shall soon see.

While the term is normally used in reference to academic outcomes, namely standardized test scores and math and reading levels, it is just as applicable to graduation and drop-out rates, disciplinary infractions, absenteeism [24], and socioeconomic outcomes. With regard to academic outcomes and standardized tests, specifically, below are the SAT results for the classes of 1997, 2007 and 2017, respectively (scores out of a possible 1600):

1997	2007	2017
All – 1015	1020	1060
Asian – 1060	1090	1180
White – 1050	1060	1120
Hisp/Latino – 915	920	990
Black – 860	860	940

[25]

As you can see, there exists a clear and persistent gap, over a twenty-year span, of Asian and White scores being consistently stronger than Hispanic and African-American scores: an *achievement gap*, if you will. And while the results are plain for all to see, the root causes are a bit more opaque, hidden, and obstructed from view. But alas dear reader, we are nothing if not adventurous, right? So let us now delve a little deeper into some of the reasons behind this stubborn and persistent delta.

Chapter 2:

Your Neighborhood, Your School

High school is a formative time for everyone. That goes for the cool kids, the shy kids, the rich kids, the poor kids, the theatre geeks, the nerds, the jocks, the goths, the knuckleheads, those just trying to get by without being seen, those trying way too hard to be seen, and everyone in between. Even those students that are acutely aware of all those tired archetypes who, try as they might to avoid them, end up falling into one or more eventually. So it is, so it was, so it will more than likely always be. But regardless of wherever a student finds themselves within the given social hierarchy of their school, the academic template of what's available to them -from day one of their high school experience- is there for all to see: the school profile.

A school profile is essentially a breakdown of the type of institution that a particular school is. It can contain such information as demographic statistics, academic systems and summaries, graduation requirements, grading scale information, extra-curricular offerings, etc. Profiles are a required part of an application at many colleges and universities as it helps to give context to a particular applicant's transcript and test scores. It's how universities evaluate how academically rigorous a particular student's time was in high school.

Did they take advantage of the resources available at their school? If the school offers College Prep, Honors, AP, or IB courses did the student challenge themselves by taking some; or did they simply coast along a general academic track? What is the college going culture: expected, or the exception? Is the school a "test factory"? If so, what does that say for the particular score of the applicant you are currently evaluating (as an Admission Counselor), within the context of that school? Is the school located in an urban or suburban location? Is it in a rural locale? If you're reading between the lines, school profiles also speak to the socioeconomic realities at play for a particular school.

From my experience, visiting high schools coast-to-coast, every fall and spring for the last fifteen years, there are essentially three categories or types of high schools: publics, privates, and public-privates. The differences can be both stark and subtle, minimal and significant. The main difference between publics and privates, by definition, is funding and cost; with publics receiving funds from federal, state, and local sources, and privates being funded, in large part, by endowments and private donors. So obviously, there are, generally speaking, stark socioeconomic differences at play for such institutions. Public-Privates, as I will refer to them, indicate those institutions that are in fact public, yet due to the zip code in which they are located are able to access as many resources as most private institutions; including, but not limited to, multiple college counselors instead of one, if any. Additionally, these schools may never face the threat of closing an entire athletic department, or specific sports or arts program, due to funding. And their college attainment rates and academic profiles can be as strong as, or stronger than, many private schools. All of which are points we will circle back to in a moment.

Now, in my opinion, the academic formula for success in high school is relatively simple: (1) Go to school; (2) Pay attention; (3) Do the work. What complicates things, however, is whether or not you have the *resources and fortitude* to combat all that life can and may throw at you along the way –peer pressure, insecurity, drug or alcohol abuse (they usually go hand in hand), physical or sexual abuse, divorce, death, money issues, mental issues, learning disabilities, bullying, gang pressures or violence, illness, incarceration, hunger, homelessness, etc.— and to what extent you are faced with these challenges, if at all.

For some, there is a constant juggling act between school and several of these distractions. For others, they are foreign concepts that only others experience. No one is immune to these pressures, regardless of income or social status. But for those on the lower end of things, socioeconomically speaking at least, there is an exponentially higher likelihood that at least some of these pressures consume a greater amount of their time and energy on a daily basis.

And so, with regard to the first step in our academic formula —attendance— are you able to be present in the classroom from day to day? Or do you struggle with the ability to make it to and from school on a regular basis due to any of those pressures? As for the second, are you able to pay attention or study, either in the classroom or at home? Do you take good notes in class? Do you go home and review those notes: nightly, weekly, and before tests? Or do you have too many real and important distractions around you that draw your focus elsewhere? For the third, do you complete and turn in your homework? Do you finish class assignments? Do you do the work of being a student? Or does the actual work of a part-time job, raising siblings, or maintaining a household, consume your time away from the classroom or your attention when in it?

It is the extent to which these external pressures are allowed to complicate that simplistic academic formula, which will determine, in large part, a student's ability to do well and thrive in high school; or elementary, middle school or college, for that matter. The truly exceptional students are those who have the mental fortitude and personal grit, the *"ganas,"* as my colleague refers to it, to overcome those challenges when faced with them, and *still* maintain their focus and determination to achieve academically. Those are the success stories everyone celebrates, that we hear about in the news and on talk shows and podcasts. Rightfully so, because their examples are so few and far between in *the grand scheme of things*. And that, my friends, is no coincidence.

Circling back to our initial discussion of the three types of high schools as I have defined them -publics, privates, and public-privates- it is worth beginning with a general sense of how things actually *look* in the average American public high school. And for all intents and purposes, that picture is either very black and or white, predominantly brown, or, in certain pockets of the West Coast, at least, very Asian. The state of things in our high schools are, increasingly instead of decreasingly, very segregated; even more so than in past generations.

How could this be, one might ask? How could American schools today be as divided and segregated as they once were by mandate? How, after more than fifty years since *Brown vs. Board of Education* could this still be the case? Well the answer is pretty simple: it's by design.

You see, as mentioned before, public schools receive funding from three main sources: federal, state, and local revenues. Nationally, on average, about eight percent of this funding comes from the federal government, with forty-seven percent coming from state sources, and forty-five percent coming from local sources. [26] Those percentages can and do vary from state to state. In California, for example, for the 2014-15 academic year, state revenues accounted for fifty-seven percent of public school funding, while local revenues accounted for twenty-seven percent. Here's the kicker, for that same year, nationally, eighty-one percent of local funding for K-12 schools came from local property taxes. [27] Now you don't have to be a genius to realize the implications of what this means for richer versus poorer areas, in terms of revenue generation, and therefore access to resources.

You also don't have to be a history major to know that race relations in this country have a very complicated past. But you might have to do a little digging in the archives in order to realize that our very own government has played a central role in the creation of those richer versus poorer areas, all while intentionally maintaining racial division. As the preeminent scholar on the subject, Richard Rothstein, explains:

> School segregation is primarily a problem of neighborhoods, not schools. Schools are segregated because

the neighborhoods in which they are located are segregated....

We have adopted a national myth that neighborhoods are

segregated "de facto"; i.e., because of income differences,

individual preferences, a history of private discrimination, etc.

In fact, neighborhoods in New York City are segregated

primarily because of a 20th century history of deliberate public

policy to separate the races, residentially, implemented by the

city, state, and federal governments.... Such policies were

pursued by government in every region and metropolitan area

in the nation. [28]

Again, in case you missed it, "Such policies were pursued

by government in every region and metropolitan area in the

nation." Let that sink in. Not just the South, but the North, West,

East, and every municipality in between. Because while *Brown*

vs. the Board of Education had legal implications for public

accommodations such as buses, schools, lunch counters and

water fountains, among other things, it had very little impact, if

any, on private accommodations such as housing, and the

development of entire suburban tracts; even those funded with public monies. Don't believe me? Sound too far-fetched to be true? The following are excerpts from the 1936 Federal Housing Authority (FHA) Underwriting Manual:

> 228. Deed restrictions are apt to prove more effective than a zoning ordinance in **providing protection from adverse influences.** . . . It must be realized that **deed restrictions, to be effective, must be enforced**. In this respect they are like zoning ordinances. Where there is the possibility of voiding the deed restrictions through inadequate enforcement of their provisions, the restrictions themselves **offer little or no protection against adverse influences**. [29]

> 229. The geographical position of a location may afford in certain instances reliable protection against adverse influences.... **Natural or artificially established barriers (*such as waterways, interstates, freeways, or railroad tracks*) will prove effective in protecting a neighborhood** and the locations within it from adverse influences. Usually the protection against adverse influences afforded by these means include **prevention of** the infiltration of business and industrial uses, **lower-class occupancy, and inharmonious racial groups**. [30 *The information in italics is added for clarity*]

> 233. The Valuator should investigate areas surrounding the location to **determine whether or not incompatible racial and social groups are present**, to the end that an intelligent prediction may be made regarding the possibility or probability of the location **being invaded by such groups**. If a neighborhood is to retain stability it is *necessary* that properties shall **continue to be occupied by the same social and racial classes**. A change in social or racial occupancy **generally leads to instability and a reduction in values**. [31]

> .... **The social class of the parents of children at the school** will in many instances have a vital bearing. Thus, although physical surrounds of a neighborhood area may be favorable and

conducive to enjoyable, pleasant living in its locations, if the children of people living in such an area are compelled to attend school where the majority or a goodly number of the pupils **represent a far lower level of society or an incompatible racial element**, the neighborhood under consideration will prove far less stable and desirable than if this condition did not exist. In such an instance it might well be that **for the payment of a fee (*private schools*) children of this area could attend another school with pupils of their same social class**. The question for the Valuator to determine is the effect created by the necessity for making this payment upon the occupants of the location. Under any conditions the rating could not be favorable as if the desirable school were available without additional cost. In many instances where a school has earned a prestige through the class of pupils attending, it will be found that such prestige will be a vital element in **maintaining the desirability** of the entire area comprising the school district. [32]

It is important to acknowledge and understand that I do not include this information simply to bring up our sordid past or further divide us as citizens. That is not the point of this discussion in the least. I bring up these points because although racial attitudes and relations have undoubtedly -for the most part- improved ten-fold from eighty years ago, these federal, state, and local policies and their implications on future generations leading on up to the present have *never* been fully acknowledged or addressed. And so we continue to see their effects on our communities and schools, creating and maintaining -institutionalizing, if you will- the dreaded Achievement Gap, allowing no way for it to ever truly be diagnosed and hence treated. Again, this ain't rocket science, folks. If you intentionally and consistently exclude certain populations from accessing opportunities for advancement and wealth creation, i.e., home ownership, upward social mobility, etc., then there will be a persistent and insurmountable gap between those with and those without.

For those of you who contend that there's no way this injustice has been allowed to persist for the past eighty years, you're half right. In 1968 Congress passed the —for the most part toothless— Fair Housing Act, which did indeed eliminate the most blatant forms of literal discrimination utilized by government agencies, yet lacked any enforcement provisions for the first 20 years of its existence; opting instead, to promise the investigation of housing discrimination complaints and "engage in conference, conciliation, and persuasion to resolve the problem" *if* discrimination was found to be present. [33] All bark and no bite, as it were.

The result, as Wayne State University Professor, James Carr, reported in a 2018 Forbes article, is that the African-American homeownership rate is essentially what it was in 1968, forty-two and forty-seven percent of blacks and Hispanics own their homes compared to seventy-three percent of whites, and people of color are several times more likely to be denied access to loans, the victims of predatory loans, or forced to meet unreasonable requirements to secure loans. [34] All of which, as was stated earlier, has real consequence on the composition of black, white, and brown neighborhoods, and the schools found therein.

As Emma Brown reported in a Washington Post article from 2016:

> The proportion of schools segregated by race and class —where more than 75 percent of children receive free or reduced-price lunch, and more than 75 percent are black and

Hispanic— climbed from 9 percent to 16 percent of schools between 2001 and 2014. The number of the most intensively segregated schools —with more than 90 percent of low-income students and students of color— more than doubled over that period. [35]

And as Richard Rothstein stated in a different Washington Post article later that same year:

Today, nearly half of all black students attend majority black schools, with over 70 percent in high-poverty school districts. New York is the most segregated state: two-thirds of its black students attend schools that are less than 10 percent white. [36]

So you see, the system is not broken by any means. It is working exactly the way it was intended to. The Achievement Gap, both educationally and socioeconomically, is not a matter of happenstance or coincidence. It is not the fault of black and brown children, nor the result of innate white or Asian intellectual superiority. It is a product of social design.

Still, from my vantage point at least, the single best tool for fighting this systemic oppression, at both the individual level and en masse, is educational attainment. Educational attainment, and the advancement it promises, is a far better bet than hitting the lottery, playing professional sports, becoming an entertainer, or getting one million Youtube views or Instagram followers. It's a much safer and healthier decision than living a life of crime. And at the K-12 level it's compensatory: meaning you have to go to school anyway. So why not make the best of it? The system is not designed for the sweeping success and upward mobility of the masses; white, black, or any ethnicity in between. By definition there must be a lower-class if there is to be a middle and upper-class. But even if the odds continue to be stacked against you, at least now you know the rules. And the more educated you become the better you can play the game; because it's chess, not checkers.

Chapter 3:

The State of Higher Ed

For the fall 2018 academic year, there were 15.1 million students in grades 9 through 12 nationally; with less than 2 million attending private schools. [37] That included some 4 million incoming public high school freshmen, an estimated 3.3 million public high school seniors in the Class of 2019, and an additional 0.4 million private high school seniors. [38] For about a ten year period, from 2017 to the mid-2020's, the number of secondary students is expected to rise. But things will take a somewhat drastic turn after that, in part due to a prolonged period of reduced fertility rates in young American adults, referred to as a *birth-dearth*, which began shortly after the Great Recession of '08.

In fact, immediately following the Great Recession, birth-rates in the country fell thirteen percent in just 5 years as Americans were more hesitant to begin families in uncertain economic times. [39] In his book, *Demographics and the Demand for Higher Education*, economist and author, Nathan Grawe, asserts that the impacts of this birth-dearth will really begin to take shape around the year 2026, primarily through shrinking recruitment pools for colleges, as evidenced in a fifteen to twenty percent drop in Northeast high school graduates alone. [40] Additionally, from about 2015 until 2025, the country will experience a drop in white and black high school graduates, while the number of Asian graduates will see a solid increase. [41] The percentage-share of some student populations, namely Asian and Hispanic / Latino, will increase during the dip. But it will not be enough to offset the overall plunge in the number of students. [42] And while all this might not mean much to high school students, believe me, colleges and universities are already preparing for this eventuality.

So the question remains: what is the current state of higher education in America? I would contend that it is one of soul searching; of trying to find a new and better, more efficient way of doing things, of trying to maintain homeostasis and relevance in an ever more volatile, and in some ways adverse landscape, of attempting to justify what is rapidly approaching, in some circles, close to an $80,000 a year proposition. For better or for worse, technology has changed the game. And while it has yet to become the great-equalizer that many envisioned it would, it has helped to shed light on many of the flaws in our current educational system. On one hand, in an age of instant gratification and instantaneous access to knowledge once only found in stodgy old libraries -in actual physical books, no less- many have come to question the necessity of the institution of college altogether; the stresses of applying and being rejected, the time spent on general education requirements instead of career focused coursework, the increasing time to degree completion and therefore the increased amount of time out of the workforce, the growing costs of attaining an education, the accumulation of debt, an assumed *liberal* (or educated) ideological entrenchment, etc. And on the other, colleges and universities themselves are finding it increasingly more difficult to go on with business as usual as fixed-costs such as infrastructure –the actual building and maintaining of buildings– and faculty salaries, along with decreasing enrollments and high-discount rates continue to wreak havoc on what was once a very stable business model.

All things considered, however, for the time being, and for the foreseeable future if we're to be honest with ourselves, college is and will remain the best and most accessible option for advancement on both an individual level and for the masses. Again, look at the statistics. Educational attainment, and the correlated employment opportunities that come along with it, have allowed two relatively small groups of ethnic minorities to become socioeconomic powerhouses in this country: Indian and Asian Americans.

When discussing the state of higher education, I find it useful to have a sense of the number and varying types of institutions involved in the conversation. According to the National Center for Education Statistics (NCES), which as its website states, is the "primary federal entity for collecting and analyzing data related to education in the U.S. and other nations," [43] in the year 2012 there were 4,495 degree granting institutions: 2,774 four-year colleges and 1,721 two-year colleges. A lot of options; far more schools than any one student could ever, or should ever, attempt to apply to. And those figures may have shifted slightly since 2012 as a growing number of schools, both public and private, two-year and four-year, have been forced to either merge with other institutions or have closed their doors altogether. As the financial analytics company, Moody's, reports, "Closures among four-year public and private not-for-profit colleges averaged five per year from 2004-14, while mergers averaged two to three." [44] Still, there are many many potential next stops for the graduating high school senior.

According to the National Student Clearinghouse, which tracks ninety-seven percent of college enrollment nationwide across all postsecondary institutions [45], 44.8% of the fall 2012 cohort began their education at a public four-year institution. About a third of all college students (33%) for that same year began at a public two-year school. And only about twenty percent of the cohort attended four-year not-for-profit private schools. [46] Now what's important to note here is that the fall 2012 cohort can actually be read as "the graduating Class of 2018," as it is now common-place, and has been for some years, for schools to report six-year graduation rates as opposed to four-year rates. Perhaps that's because the national four-year graduation rate is a lowly forty-one percent overall, with some of the larger research schools coming in at an abysmal nineteen percent. [47] The national six-year rate, however, is closer to sixty percent (58.3%); with four-year privates topping the group with a seventy-six percent six-year grad rate. [48]

For the fall 2018 cohort, there were nearly 20 million students projected to attend American colleges and universities. [49] And as stated above, as things currently stand, the majority of all college students attend four-year public schools, such as the University of California (UC) and California State University (CSU) system in California, the New York University system, or the state school systems of Arizona. Every state has at least one publicly funded school system, and some have more than one; Texas has six, which is a bit excessive if you ask me, but apparently everything is bigger in Texas.

I find it easier and much simpler to break down the myriad number of four-year options into three distinct categories: Liberal Arts colleges, Comprehensive Universities, and research-focused state schools and Flagship Institutions, which are usually public. I also find that it is usually more effective when describing these options to students and families, to speak of the different types of schools in terms of their relative sizes, and the potential realities, academically and socially, of each.

Liberal Arts Colleges

The key terms here are "small and broad." Small in the sense of the population of most liberal arts colleges, which range from a few hundred to around 4 or 5,000. The proximity to opportunities and professors are a big selling-point, or positive, for these institutions. Average class sizes at liberal arts colleges can range from less than ten to around twenty-five on the high-end. Student to faculty ratios are usually in the single digits or teens to one.

For context, many public high schools in California and Texas have populations of at least 1,200 students, and it's not much of a rarity in many states to have high schools in excess of 3,000 students or more. The average public high school class size in California is thirty-five students. So these four-year liberal arts colleges are as small as, or smaller, than most public high schools, with much smaller class sizes, much smaller student to faculty ratios, and in comparison to many colleges and universities, much higher four year graduation rates, usually.

Now small class sizes are a consideration I think more students, especially more underrepresented and first-generation students, or students from lower socioeconomic backgrounds, should seriously weigh in their decision-making. And I say that from two perspectives: preparation and confidence. In terms of preparation, underrepresented or poorer students are more likely to show up to college having come from a large and often under-resourced public high school. They are less likely to have already had the experience of being in a class small enough to have actually allowed for substantive classroom discussion, or Socratic teaching methods, and are therefore either actually less prepared to do so, or incorrectly assume that they are. That is where the issue of confidence in their own abilities to flourish in such an environment come into play; i.e., the Imposter Syndrome, essentially, questioning whether or not they actually deserve to be where they are. And confidence in your abilities is key. This is a truism in every context, for sure, but a necessity in smaller classroom settings. A student needs to have the confidence in him or herself to know that they can hang and perform with their private school peers. Which they can, more often than not, once they've adjusted.

In smaller environments there is also a greater chance for students to do *undergraduate* research alongside their professors (who have to continue in their own scholarship but do not have graduate students to rely on), to get published, have access to an internship, study abroad, and have the ability to do all of the important networking one should be doing in college. Thus, the higher price-tag as liberal arts colleges are usually private. As they say, "You get what you pay for." And you are paying for that access and opportunity! The dreaded term *impaction* should never be a reality at a liberal arts college. Or at the very least, it will be a short-lived one once those alumni parents and donors catch wind. Impaction, by the way, meaning over-crowding and unavailability; as in the unavailability of a particular class, major, school, or entire university within a college system. The results of impaction tend to lead to delayed degree completion and lower graduation rates.

The flip-side of attending schools this small is, potentially, limited resources due to that small size. The "broad" nature of many liberal arts majors can equate to a lack of specificity in what students are able to study. For example, while a student at a large research university may have the opportunity to be a specific type of Biology major (marine, biochem, micro, ecology, entomolgy, etc.), students at liberal arts colleges are usually just Biology majors, with an area of emphasis, perhaps.

Ever heard of a 3-2 program? That usually describes a system where a liberal arts college partners up with larger research schools and has a student study physics –usually– at their institution for three years, then sends the student off to one of the aforementioned universities for an additional two years, studying Engineering, and completing the process with one or two Bachelor's degrees; not a Master's.

Socially, smaller environments can sometimes feel a little too intimate, stifling even, for some students. News travels fast, gossip even faster. And it spreads like wildfire in an environment of 1,500 as opposed to 15 or 30,000; and that was before the advent of social media. Thus, there are some drawbacks, aside from cost, to smaller environments.

Flagship / Research Universities

Now you're playing with the big boys! In terms of size, these are the largest schools around. These usually public institutions are indeed so large because they were founded as land-grant, publicly-funded institutions of higher learning, with the intent of being accessible to as many qualified students, primarily from their given state, as possible. In California, for example, we have the CSU and UC systems; the UC's being the higher tier of the two. As I write this, UCLA, UC Berkeley, UC Santa Barbara, UC Irvine, UC Davis, and UC Riverside are among the Top 10 public schools in the nation according to the 2019 Best Colleges rankings of US News and World Report, with the universities of Virginia, Michigan, North Carolina at Chapel Hill, and Georgia Tech rounding out the group; the University of Florida and the College of William and Mary make the list as well tied at number 8 and 10, respectively. [50]

Size-wise, we're talking student populations of twenty to 50,000 and up. Arizona State University is currently the largest institution in the country at nearly 80,000 students on its physical campuses alone; they are around 130,000 students if you count their online enrollment. And yes, those numbers include both undergrad and graduate students, as they should, because graduate student Teaching Assistants are a common reality in the classrooms of many of these institutions as the professors often find themselves immersed in the very research for which these schools were founded. So as a lowly undergrad student, you can forget about substantive classroom discussion or 1 on 1 meetings with said professor.

However, in all fairness, if you're the kind of student that can take great notes, go *home* to your dorm room, library, coffee shop, or quiet space, study those notes, then come into class and ace a test, you'll do fine academically in such an environment. Some students attend very small high schools and look forward to the anonymity afforded to students at large campuses where class attendance is not a part of one's grade. As the individual in charge of the transfer process at my current institution, I've been able to get a good sense of the average introductory class sizes at most public schools. By introductory classes I'm referring to the general education type courses in English, Math, or Science that everyone at a given institution must complete. From my experience, it is safe to say that these classes are usually in the range of 300 to 400 students. They can be much larger than that, however. The largest classes I've ever heard of, in person -meaning I've met with or read the application of a student attempting to transfer out of such situations- were 1,500 and 1,700, respectively; both were introductory Biology classes.

Additionally, with larger institutions there are sometimes more stringent criteria needed in order to declare a particular major on a given campus. You may have been admitted into a particular school or college within that large university, but you may also find that it is harder than you initially thought to have the particular major you want.

Socially, you will typically find a large Greek Life presence on large campuses. And this makes total sense. When you are in an academic environment of such large classes, and the dog-eat-dog competitive nature of said classes which are usually graded on a curve, you're not really able to make friends or even social connections all that easily. I've read essays where students describe the isolated feelings of never seeing a familiar face outside of the classroom; a potential reality that comes with a campus of 40,000 plus students. So Greek Life moves in to fill that void. On some campuses you'll find Greek Life participation in the fifty to eighty percent range, because that's how you get to know people. It becomes the mandate socially, as opposed to an option, as it is on smaller campuses.

If you're a sports fan, or you like strong school spirit, then a big school might be just what you're looking for. Football and Basketball reign supreme on these campuses, and in the NCAA in general, as the revenues from those two sports alone fund virtually all other sports. Personally, while I never attended a large institution, this is an aspect of them –the sports history and tradition– that I find very appealing. There's something electric about college football Saturdays and March Madness brackets; the tailgating and mixture of proud alums, the generations of families supporting their alma mater, etc. It's undeniably fun, and altogether alluring as a potential student. Believe me, I get it.

In the end, I think there are arguments to be made for both small and large institutions with respect to which type of institution best prepares students for life in the *real world*. While

I think the competitive dog-eat-dog nature of life on a large campus does foster a sink or swim attitude and fortitude in students, qualities undoubtedly necessary for adult survival, I also see value in the many ways smaller schools allow students to interact and network with other students, professors and administration. As the age old axiom goes, "it's not always about what you know, sometimes it's about who you know." And smaller environments simply allow students the opportunity to get to know more people in real and meaningful ways.

Additionally, I think there is an academic benefit for some students to be in smaller environments; if they can afford it. Probably the biggest drawback to smaller schools is the price-tag. Again, if you want access you usually have to pay for it. And how much debt one should be willing to go into for a Bachelor's degree, or college education in general, will always be a raging debate. But in that respect, in most cases, even with scholarships and financial aid factored in, public schools have a definite leg-up on cost. In the end, as it quite often does and usually should, I think the conversation comes down to fit; does school "X" fit a student's needs, means, and abilities, educationally, socially, financially, etc.

Comprehensive / Master's Universities

Comprehensive Universities are essentially a middle-ground between Liberal Arts Colleges and research schools, both in terms of size, usually, and academic programming. Grounded in a liberal arts philosophy, comprehensive schools usually allow for a more flexible and well-rounded academic experience; as opposed to a curriculum purely grounded in a specific program, i.e., business, the natural sciences, the arts, or engineering. Population-wise, I'd say most schools of this sort fall within the 5 to 20,000 total students range; which isn't small enough to feel smothering, but also not large enough to get lost in. There isn't much more to add to the concept of comprehensive institutions, other than that you will probably find a positive correlation to smaller overall student populations and retention and completion rates.

The First Stop is not always the Last Stop: Transferring

In the fall of 2011, 2.8 million first-time students entered a college campus. Within the next six years these same students made over 1 million transitions from one school to another. [51] Now, as explained before, the fall class of 2011 can be better understood as the graduating Class of 2017, as it is now commonplace to discuss college as a six-year, as opposed to four-year, endeavor. Indeed, it is common practice for institutions to report a six-year graduation rate as opposed to a four-year rate. So always ask for *specificity* in the statistics you're told.

What this study reports is that during the six years that the Class of 2017 was in college, for the 2.8 million students that started in 2011, there were over 1 million transfers made. In all, thirty-eight percent of students transferred at least once. The directionality of those transfers could make one dizzy as students went from four-years to two-years, two-years to four years, four-years to four-years, four-years to two-years back to four-years, etc. All of which is completely understandable as many students will start out at a given four-year institution, but not be ready for the adjustment academically, mentally, maturation-wise, you name it, and will therefore have to transition to a two-year in order to get *back on their feet*, as it were. At which point transferring to a different four-year, or returning to the original, would then be the goal.

As for two-year, or Community College students, the goal of most two-year students is to eventually transition to a four-year school. So that transition also makes total sense. Unfortunately, only around a quarter of all Community College students go on to transfer to a four-year school. [52] At this point, I think we have to pause and recognize that something is wrong when an educational system intended to be a stepping-stone to grander pastures, is only successful in matriculating twenty-five percent of its students. Sure, not all students attend a Community College with aspirations of attending a four-year institution. But I'm willing to bet that that is the ideal destination for far more than a quarter of all Community College students. Just as their four-year counterparts have become a six-year endeavor, it has become commonplace to expect what used to be a two year experience to now take up to three years, as a good proportion of students enter community college at a remedial level and therefore need to make up ground before attaining transferable course work. Along those lines, it is important to note that the NSC report found that only forty-two percent of the two-year to four-year transfers attained a Bachelor's degree within the six years that the study was conducted. [53] So the takeaway there, as I see it, is both that the educational system needs to address the degree attainment discrepancy between four-year and two-year students, and also that community college students themselves need to take more onus on being focused on their degree completion.

As stated earlier, in my current role, I oversee the transfer process for my institution, and have done so for many years. Over that time I've come to realize that transfer students, no matter the particular story, generally fall into one of three categories; although they can definitely double-dip or even triple dip between them.

The first group would comprise those students who did indeed start at a community college, for any number of reasons, and thus need to transition to a four-year campus in order to complete a Bachelor's degree. The second would be those previously mentioned students that started at a four-year, and for whatever reason ended up leaving said school, heading to a community college with the hopes of one day transferring to another four-year, or heading straight to another four-year school with the hopes of it being a better fit. And the third would be any and all "non-traditional" students. And that's about it. In fact, every time I meet with a potential transfer student who begins the meeting with "I have a bit of a unique situation," it takes everything in the fibers of my being to fight a reflexive eye-roll. The take-away from all of this should simply be that transferring is normal. Anyone who stigmatizes or looks down upon the concept of it should simply get over themselves.

Period.

Chapter 4:

College Counseling 101

I guess a good place to start this part of the discussion is with the question, "Should everyone go to college?" And the answer to that, in my opinion, is no, not everyone should go to college. College isn't for everyone. Some people simply don't like or thrive in a school environment. And as long as they can find positive and gainful pursuits outside of it I have no issue with someone taking an alternate path. That said, I think everyone should be educated. As where some see college simply as a stepping-stone to better employment opportunities, I see college as a path towards a more expansive maturity and world-view. College, if anything, is an experience: a fun one, a rewarding one, an enriching one. I tell folks all the time that if you're not a genius going in, college won't make you a genius coming out. But hopefully you will have learned a few things along the way. Developed new skills, met new people, seen new places, had your beliefs and assumptions challenged, made memories that will last a lifetime, faced and overcome hard times. These are all the real and lasting benefits of a college education; not just that piece of paper at the end, although that is truly beneficial as well. It's a way-station between youth and adulthood. You're not a child anymore, but not quite a responsible adult grownup either. It is for these reasons that I believe everyone should have the option and ability to go to college should they so choose. They should have access to a higher education. And how do you ensure that access? Through preparation.

The journey to college starts on day one of freshmen year of high school. And in reality it starts much much earlier than that. But in terms of what college admission professionals can actually assess as your college readiness, as far as the classes you take and grades you receive, that journey starts on day one.

And sure, some public school systems do not evaluate freshman year grades and coursework. But let me tell you, if you haven't developed a strong study habit by your freshman year, chances are it won't magically materialize by sophomore year. So the bottom line is, take it seriously from the beginning. "It" being your future, and the maximization of your college options.

From day one take it upon yourself as a student or parent to know everything that the school offers academically. From the requirements for graduation to the most demanding and challenging classes offered. Know whether your school offers college prep, Honors, Advance Placement, or International Baccalaureate courses. Ask about the requirements to gain access to either of those options. Ask about the general guidelines for access to your state's public college and university system. In California, for example, the UC system came up with the "A-G" terminology, to indicate those high school courses that students must pass with a grade of "C" or better, in order to meet their *minimum* admission requirements; fifteen yearlong courses, eleven of which must be completed prior to the student's senior year.

Compare and contrast your high school's graduation requirements against the minimum requirements for college entry and find the areas and subject matters where you may need to go above and beyond. For example, most high schools only require three years of math. And the traditional math trajectory at the secondary level is Algebra I, Geometry, Algebra II, Pre-Calculus, then Statistics, Calculus, and higher, if offered. So when a school only requires three years of math, and a student only takes three years, that will put them at Algebra II. You would be hard pressed to find any selective institution that would consider an applicant to be viable with an Algebra II math level. Most majors within the Humanities, Liberal Arts, or the Natural and Social sciences will require at least Statistics at the college level. So why not make at least Pre-Calculus or Statistics the required level of math for graduation at the high school level?

To those students who have the means or ability to participate in dual-enrollment programs —in which students can earn college credits while still in high school— I offer this bit of advice, taking College Algebra at your local Community College in an attempt to side-step Statistics or Calculus at your high school is *not* impressive. Taking Linear Algebra at said Community College because you've completed your high school's Calculus series *is* impressive. To me, given the time and effort, as well as the disruption in one's day that traveling to and from a college campus can impose on one's schedule, I think that students should be as strategic and selective as possible when it comes to this option. Taking college courses while in high school is only impressive to me when you are going above and beyond what your high school offers. That said, I also understand the cost-effectiveness aspect of attempting to knock out some general education requirements. I get that, I really do. But I stand by the sentiment of my previous statement.

Along those lines, we live in an increasingly diverse and global society. So why not take advantage of as many years of a foreign language as you can while at the high school level? As any adult will attest to, trying to learn a foreign language, or any new skill, gets tougher the older you get. There's truth to the saying "You can't teach an old dog new tricks." And it's not that it's necessarily impossible to do so, it's simply the fact that the older you get the more life gets in the way; the more you get set in your ways. So why not take advantage of a time and space – high school– dedicated to the acquisition of such skills, and make the most of it. Some colleges and universities have a foreign language requirement of their own. So again, why not persist in a foreign language at the high school level?

As for electives and community service in high school, those things tend to take care of themselves as many schools have requirements for each these days. In terms of extra-curricular activities and being a well-rounded individual, my advice is to simply pursue what you like and what you're passionate about. If it's sports then play sports. If it's art then create art. If it's theatre, well, you get the picture. Do what you like. Do as many things as you like. But don't do something simply because you think it will look good on a college application. Bottom line, don't be boring, and don't be a lemming.

As for testing, I tell students all the time that standardized test scores do not equate to how smart or intelligent a given student is. They are hours-long tests taken on a Saturday, mostly, and there is a stronger socioeconomic correlation –stronger than race or ethnicity– in terms of who does what on those tests. Basically, those students with the means to have private tutoring, private counselors, the luxury of having test prep classes offered *at their school –as part of the curriculum–* and the ability to take the tests multiple times, tend to do better on said tests. It's that simple. But as far as testing is concerned, regardless of situation, my advice is that students should aim to take both the ACT and SAT, and they should aim to do so by the end of junior year. Once the results are in, if they feel like they can do better on either test, take it again. I never recommend a third attempt. That sounds like torture. And both anecdotally and in my experience, there is usually very little improvement on the third attempt, statistically speaking.

To the question of when should you start visiting schools, I say it's never too early! For most Americans, unless you live in a rural or isolated area, there is probably at least one college or university within a few miles to a couple of hours drive from you. Do some research. Check out what schools are close, or close enough, and get out and visit them; either officially or unofficially.

If you are a parent, and your child or children are younger, as in the elementary or middle school years, and you really just want them to get a sense of what a college campus looks and feels like, then simply walking around a college campus will suffice. But as your child gets closer to the age in which he or she may actually be attending college within a few years, then you will definitely want to take as many official college tours as possible. Not only for the child's sake, but also because colleges and universities increasingly take demonstrated interest into account during the admission process. Has the student who claims that we are number one on his or her list actually visited the campus? Do they live within a reasonable distance, travel-wise? If so, why have they not made the effort? If they did visit, what was their reaction to the people and campus? In the *guessing game* of college admission, schools want to admit students who actually demonstrate their willingness to attend.

More than that though, you want to hear information directly from the horse's mouth, as it were. In this case, that would be the Admission Counselor, faculty, staff or students of a given school. You never want to rely solely on hearsay, or what you've heard about a particular university from friends, family, acquaintances, or even counselors. Admission presentations should give you the insight you need with regards to the academic programs, application, admission and financial aid protocols and deadlines, academic stats, a sense of campus life, etc., at a particular school. Good presentations should include all of that and then some, including information coming directly from students at that school. Most, if not all institutions, offer information sessions and tours at least weekly or throughout the week; some even on weekends. Most are free. You just have to find the time to make it happen.

Your goal should simply be to get out and see as many campuses as you can. Preferably while school is in session. But in reality, whenever you can visit you should. And check out different types of schools: small schools, big schools, medium-sized schools, public, private, religiously affiliated, and community colleges. Going on a road trip for a family vacation? Stop by a local college or a university on the way.

If you, as the parent or provider, did not attend college and are simply trying to figure things out as you go, then by all means start this process as early as possible. If you or your spouse or partner did attend college, then starting with either of your alma maters makes perfect sense; preferably the one with the better football or basketball team. The point is to get the student familiar and comfortable with the *idea* of college and of *going to college,* as soon as possible. A task which will be easier for some than others, but at least now you know the steps to take to begin that process.

To the notion of the necessity of hiring a private or independent counselor to assist you in this process, I say this: the concept of private counselors is a lot like the concept of the food delivery service DoorDash. For those who can afford it and are either too busy, too lazy, well-intentioned but uninterested in the process, or simply unaware of their options, the hiring of an Independent Counselor, just like employing the services of DoorDash, makes perfect sense. For individuals or families with the means to do so, it is always easier to let someone else handle the dirty work.

The reality is that independent, private counselors or educational consultants, whichever term you prefer, are unnecessary. Especially in the day and age of the all-knowing, all-powerful, omnipresent Google. Yet we live in a society of self-driving cars, refrigerators that tell us when to buy groceries, transportation on demand through services like Lyft and Uber, and battery powered self-propelling skateboards and scooters. None of which is necessary. All of which makes our lives easier. The irony of the situation is that most families that can afford to pay for an Independent Counselor are already sending their child to a private school; an institution well-equipped and staffed to give their student the exact kind and quality of direction that they are searching for.

Those with the ability to do so will usually take whatever means possible to simplify their life. Ours is not a society based upon essential needs. Ours is a society obsessed with access and ease. Give me what I want now, and with as little effort as is humanly possible. In such an environment, independent counselors definitely make sense: potentially many tens of thousands of dollars and cents.

That said, if you were paying attention, I just told you everything you need to know in order to be successful in the college search process. Don't believe me? Let's put it to the test.

A Case Study

Let us now take a look at the school profiles of three San Jose, California (my hometown) high schools, and discuss what an applicant would need to do at each particular school in order to be competitive in most college or university applicant pools. We will focus on competitiveness for medium to highly-selective institutions, as most state university systems have clear-cut admission requirements.

James Lick High School (school profile below)

JAMES LICK HIGH SCHOOL

57 NORTH WHITE ROAD, SAN JOSE, CALIFORNIA, 95127 · TELEPHONE: (408) 347-4400 · FAX: (408) 347-4415

Established in 1950, James Lick High School is a comprehensive, four-year, public, coeducational, urban high school. It is the smallest of the 11 comprehensive high schools in the East Side Union High School District with approximately 1150 students.

Accreditation: Accreditation has been granted by the Western Association of Schools and Colleges.

Grading Scale:

Letter Grade	Grade Points	
A	4.00	I - Incomplete (Becomes F if not made up)
B	3.00	Exception: Summer school grades range
C	2.00	from A to D with a U
D	1.00	for audit. F grades are not given for ESUHSD
F	0.00	Summer School.

Graduation Requirements:

A minimum of 220 credits is required for graduation. Ten credits equal one year of work for one period.

Subject	Credits
English	40
Mathematics (Min. Algebra 1 and Geometry or Math I and Math II)	20
Science - (Min. 1 Biological and 1 Physical Science)	20
Social Science	30
Foreign Language / Fine Art	10
Physical Education	20
Electives	80

College Preparatory Classes: The letter "P-" before a class indicates it is a college preparatory class as accepted by the University of California, e.g. P-English 1, P-U.S. History, etc.

Higher Education: For the 2017-2018 school year, 45% of our students qualified for four-year colleges and universities while 1 out of every 2 graduates planned on attending community college or higher. The remaining students are pursuing trade or technical schools, the military, adult education, or joining the workforce.

Advanced Placement Courses

English Language AP	English Literature AP
Calculus AB AP	Government & Politics AP
Spanish Language AP	Spanish Literature AP
World History AP	US History AP
Studio Art 2D AP	Psychology AP
Chemistry AP + Lab AP	Biology AP + Lab AP
Computer Science AP	

Fire Service Magnet Program: Since 2013, the Fire Service Program graduates receive CPR certification and EMT Test Preparation. This program prepares students who have a career goal in the medical, fire, or emergency service areas. It requires leadership training and community service hours. It is not college preparatory.

Telephone Numbers for Guidance Staff

Mrs. Llanos-Richards - Head Counselor (408) 347-4448
Ms. Chavez - Counselor (408) 347-4443
Mr. Steven Loya - Counselor (408) 347-4446
Ms. Veronica Vasquez - Counselor (408) 347-4474
Ms. Debra Guzman - Counseling Tech. (408) 347-4442
Ms. Enriqueta Alvarez - Registrar (408) 347-4421

Transcript Notations: Class Rank and GPA - Class rank is based on the cumulative GPA. All classes attempted are included. No classes are weighted; GPA and class rank are re-calculated periodically.

Athletic Participation: James Lick is a member of the Blossom Valley Athletic League, Santa Teresa, and West Valley Divisions.

A NEW TECH SCHOOL

Thelma Guevara	David Porter	Noemi Ramirez
Associate Principal	Principal	Associate Principal

EAST SIDE UNION HIGH SCHOOL DISTRICT - Chris Funk, Superintendent

It is the policy of the East Side Union High School District not to discriminate on the basis of sex, age, religion, race, national origin, sexual orientation or handicapping condition in its educational programs and activities or in the recruitment and employment of personnel. A NEW TECH SCHOOL

Let's get things started with my alma mater. Now as you can see from the profile, at 1,150 students James Lick is actually the smallest of the eleven high schools in the East Side Union High School district of San Jose, California. It's safe to say that most of the other schools average around 2,000 students. In fact, during my time at James Lick, the population was closer to a little over 1,200.

With regard to the current student body of James Lick, however, what this particular school profile leaves out is the demographic information of its population. Good thing for us though, this optional information is provided in the accompanying documentation -provided by the school's counselors- that comes with the school profile. For the senior class of 2017, the ethnic breakdown was as follows: 74% Hispanic / Latino, 17% Asian, 5% White, 2% Black or African-American, and 1% American Indian or Alaskan Native and Native American or Pacific Islander, respectively.

For the 243 seniors in the graduating class, thirty percent were headed to a four-year school, while fifty percent intended to go the two-year route. Eighty percent of the class were First-Generation students. And eighty percent of the class qualified for free or reduced lunch based on Federal standards. So right off the bat, as a seasoned reader of college applications and school profiles, I can see that both the demographic and college-going information speak to some of the socioeconomic realities at play for this particular school. And while this information is particular to the senior class, it is safe to expect these trends to be consistent for the James Lick population as a whole.

Why is that important, or something that a College Admission professional might take into consideration? Well, it speaks to the potential college readiness of a particular applicant from this school, as well as the overall college-going culture of the school. Is college the expected outcome for a James Lick student or the exception? For four-year school attendance, at least, it would seem that it is the exception.

Focusing back on what the school profile actually does include, you'll notice that it reports that forty-five percent of the graduating class actually qualified for enrollment at a four-year school, with half the class opting for the two-year route. Again, all of this simply helps to solidify a picture of the educational attainment expectations at James Lick.

What the profile does indicate is that James Lick grades on an A-F, 4.0 unweighted scale. It ranks its students. It offers 13 Advanced Placement courses, and students must accumulate 220 credits in order to graduate. That breakdown being: 4 years of English, *2 years of Math*, 2 years of science, 3 years of a social science, 1 year of a foreign language or fine art, and 8 electives over the four years.

Let's take a moment to recognize that only 2 years of Math are required for graduation; most schools that I'm aware of require at least 3, equating to Algebra II completion. As previously discussed, the normal Math trajectory at most high schools is Algebra 1, Geometry, Algebra II, Pre-Calculus.

Generally speaking, for most selective colleges and universities, and for most majors in a given Liberal Arts college, college-level Statistics is the base level of Math required. If a student is aiming for any major in the sciences, Business, or Engineering, then Calculus is usually preferred, if not required. Now James Lick may take the "Integrated Math" approach, in which several mathematical disciplines are combined in a given course. But still, 2 years of Math preparation at the high school level does not make for a very competitive applicant.

James Lick does offer 13 AP courses. And among those is Calculus AB. Why is that important? Because while only 2 years of Math are required for graduation from the school, there is the option of going well past the basic requirements. Thus, it should be recognized when a student does exactly that. And while there are 13 AP courses to choose from, by no means would I, as an Admission Counselor, expect a single student to take most or all of them. I would however expect to see a few on the transcript of a serious applicant. Personally, I think students should stick to

Honors or Advanced coursework in the core areas such as English, Math, and the Natural and Social Sciences, only sprinkling in what I would refer to as elective courses such as AP Studio Art or Psychology if they have the freedom and capacity to do so. Advanced courses require a lot of time and energy. So students should choose wisely and keep their personal life and well-being in mind, as opposed to simply loading up on AP's because of how they think it looks to us. Work-life balance is important, even at the high school level.

So the question remains then as to what a student needs to do at James Lick, over the course of 4 years, to become an attractive college applicant? Now the James Lick profile does not include testing information, as some schools do. Quite frankly, that is completely understandable given the demographics of the student population and the fact that, on the whole, the average standardized test scores for the school are probably nothing to boast about. But that is an important piece of the academic puzzle which needs to be accounted for in the college application process. As mentioned before there is a strong socioeconomic correlation —stronger than any other correlation— in regards to how students perform on standardized testing. That being the case, I would suggest that students at James Lick, and any other institution really, look to the free test prep resources available via the College Board, the ACT, or other resources such as Khan Academy. Sophomore year is a perfect time to start this preparation, with the intent being to officially test by junior year, and retest if possible in early senior year.

And while resources are in large part a determinant in test performance, what students do have control over is the way in which they apply themselves to their schoolwork; which is most readily evident in their overall GPA. Day in and day out do they pay attention? Do they complete and turn in their homework? Do they take good notes in class? Do they then go home and study those notes? Do they perform well when tested on the material? Do they challenge themselves with Honors and

Advanced classes at their high school if they're offered? That is what they can control. That is well within their abilities should they choose to apply themselves, regardless of family situation; although there is no denying that some family and financial situations are incredibly taxing on the student's ability to do such things. There is also no denying that those types of family and financial situations are more widespread and pervasive at schools with a student population such as James Lick, or Mount Pleasant, Independence, Yerba Buena, Oakland Tech, Richmond High, Manual Arts, Compton High School, etc.

With all this in mind, a student entering James Lick as a dewy-eyed exuberant freshman, with aspirations of attaining a *Bachelor's degree or Bust*, should at the very least aim to be in Statistics by senior year; as college Statistics is the math level necessary for most majors within a particular College of Arts and Sciences. If the student has aspirations of studying anything Business or Engineering related then Calculus should be the goal. And if, as was previously stated, the average high school

Math track puts one at Pre-Calc by senior year, then that means there will need to be some summer school or course acceleration involved at some point. I'd advise knocking it out freshman or sophomore summer. If a major in the sciences is desired then continuing on past the required 2 years of science is a good plan of action. James Lick offers both AP Biology and Chemistry, for example. A student considering Pre-Med, let's say, should have at least one if not both of those courses under their belt by senior year, with some Physics along the way for good measure.

As far as a respectable and competitive GPA is concerned for a student coming out of James Lick, although it will most definitely depend on the level of selectivity of a given college or university to which that student is applying, anything at or upwards of an unweighted (4.0 scale) 3.5 is solid, in my opinion. I hear all the time how both students and parents assume that you need a 4.0 GPA to be accepted into most schools. That is simply incorrect. I think most people would be surprised to know how many "B" and even "C" grades can be found on a transcript which ultimately has a cumulative GPA of a 3.5 or higher. Although, if you're doing the math, and you realize that there are usually six classes per semester at the high school level, and that each of those classes produces two grades on a transcript for an academic year, therefore producing at least forty-eight grades on the transcript by the end of senior year, and that on an unweighted scale an "A" is worth four points, a "B" is worth three, a "C" is worth two, and so on, you will quickly see that one could not afford to have too many B's and C's and still be in that 3.5 range. In addition, the trend of a GPA matters as well. If not consistently strong throughout, then one would want to be on an upward trend as they approached senior year. Given application deadlines, junior year is typically the last year of grades a college will see.

This is not to say that a student with a 3.3, or even a 3.0, would not have some solid options as well. It is simply to say that for most competitive or selective institutions, a 3.5 or higher, in rigorous coursework, will at least give a student a fighting chance in the applicant pool.

We've already discussed my advice on the timeline of testing, but as for the desired testing level of a James Lick student, given the high concentration of First-Generation students, in addition to the socioeconomic realities at play for an institution in which eighty percent of the students are on free or reduced lunch, a score in the 1200 or above SAT is decent, which corresponds to about a 25 on the ACT. Obviously though, when it comes to testing in particular, the higher the score the better.

Generally speaking, if a James Lick student was able to achieve those standards in terms of GPA, course selection and testing, in combination with an interesting and compelling personal side, he or she would have some pretty solid college options.

Los Gatos High School (school profile below)

LOS GATOS HIGH SCHOOL

LOS GATOS-SARATOGA UNION HIGH SCHOOL DISTRICT
SCHOOL PROFILE 2017-18

ADMINISTRATION
Kristina Grasty, *Principal*
Alex Chapman, *Assistant Principal*
Amy Drolette, *Assistant Principal*
Adam Minyard, *Assistant Principal*
Protocol: firstinitiallastname@lgsuhsd.org

COUNSELORS
Farah Manganello [A-C] fmanganello@lgsuhsd.org
Louis Rich [D-F] lrich@lgsuhsd.org
Laressa Mead [G-K] lmead@lgsuhsd.org
John Benz [L-O] jbenz@lgsuhsd.org
Tamera Parks [P-Se] tparks@lgsuhsd.org
Kassandra Cochran [Si-Z] kcochran@lgsuhsd.org

ADDRESS & CONTACT INFORMATION
20 High School Court
Los Gatos, California 95030
Phone: 408.354.2730
FAX: 408.354.3742
Web Address: www.lghs.net

THE SCHOOL

Los Gatos High School is a comprehensive public high school on the southern tip of Silicon Valley. The current enrollment is approximately 2,040 students. The LGHS strategic focus goals include three major areas: relevant and engaging learning experiences; student wellness, balance and belonging; and creating a culture of collaboration and innovation. LGHS reflects the traditions, values and philosophies of its community and is proud of its robust course pathways, including honors and Advanced Placement as well as project-based, STEM-related classes such as Advanced Science Research, engineering, robotics, and "New Tech" courses. Students participate in over 70 academic, athletic and community service clubs and organizations that annually raise over $100,000 for charities and non-profit organizations. Los Gatos High School was recognized as a California Distinguished School in 2013 and is accredited by the Western Association of Schools and Colleges (WASC).

THE CURRICULUM:
ACADEMIC PROGRAM

Los Gatos High School offers academically challenging courses. Five units are awarded for each semester class. Classes meet for 90-minute periods on alternating block days. Students may take up to six classes with a seventh period available for athletics and limited course options. Grades and units are assigned in January and June. During each 18-week semester, students may take a maximum of 35 units.

GRADUATION REQUIREMENTS

SUBJECT AREA	# UNITS
ENGLISH	40
SOCIAL STUDIES	30
MATHEMATICS (INCLUDING ALGEBRA)	20
PHYSICAL EDUCATION	20
SCIENCE	20
VISUAL/PERFORMING ARTS OR WORLD LANGUAGE	10
APPLIED ARTS	5
ELECTIVES (ADDT'L CREDITS)	75
TOTAL REQUIRED UNITS:	220

GRADING

Academic weighted, four-point system, grade point average:

A = 4   B = 3   C = 2   D = 1   F = 0

- Includes all courses in grades 9-12, except PE/Sports and Teacher/Office Assistant (TA/OA)
- One extra point is given for each 9th-12th grade Honors/Advanced Placement course with a C- or higher grade.

RANKING

Los Gatos High School does not rank students.

HONORS & ADVANCED PLACEMENT COURSES

ENGLISH
English 9	[H]
English 10	[H]
English Language & Composition	[AP]
English Literature & Composition	[AP]

SOCIAL STUDIES
European History	[AP]
US History	[AP]
US Government/Politics	[AP]
Economics	[H]
Psychology	[AP]

MATHEMATICS
Trigonometry/Pre-Calculus	[H]
Calculus AB	[AP]
Calculus BC	[AP]
Statistics	[AP]

SCIENCE
Biology	[H]
Biology	[AP]
Chemistry	[AP]
Environmental Science	[AP]
Physics C: Mechanics	[AP]

WORLD LANGUAGE
French 4	[H]
French Language	[AP]
Japanese 3	[H]
Japanese Language	[AP]
Spanish 4	[H]
Spanish Language	[AP]

ELECTIVES
Computer Science	[AP]
Art 4	[H]
Music Theory	[AP]
Orchestra	[H]
Chamber Singers	[H]
Wind Ensemble	[H]

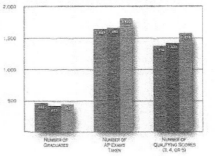

Bar chart legend: NUMBER OF GRADUATES; NUMBER OF AP EXAMS TAKEN; NUMBER OF QUALIFYING SCORES (3, 4, OR 5)

■ 2015   ■ 2016   ■ 2017

COLLEGE CHOICE
By Year of Graduation

	2015	2016	2017
2-YEAR COLLEGES	19%	23%	22%
4-YEAR COLLEGES	75%	70%	65%
TOTAL COLLEGE	94%	93%	87%

SAT REASONING DATA
Number Tested/Mean Score

	2015	2016	2017
CRITICAL READING	393/595	343/578	348/578
MATH	393/608	343/604	348/604

SAT SUBJECT DATA
Number Tested/Mean Score

EXAM SUBJECT	2015	2016	2017
LITERATURE	65/633	64/640	74/618
U.S. HISTORY	59/657	59/667	92/670
MATH LEVEL II	139/691	138/690	199/697
CHEMISTRY	16/668	7/667	22/698
PHYSICS	54/667	46/692	62/694
BIOLOGY E	27/664	16/679	17/655
BIOLOGY M	43/657	46/680	63/692
FRENCH	8/622	7/547	3/683
SPANISH	7/610	7/549	10/545

ACT DATA
Number Tested/Mean Score

EXAM SUBJECT	2015	2016	2017
ENGLISH	260/27.4	260/27.2	247/27.8
MATH	260/27.4	260/27.4	247/27.8
READING	260/27.6	260/27.2	247/27.6
SCIENCE	260/27	260/26.8	247/26.8
COMPOSITE	260/27.5	260/27.3	247/27.6

COLLEGE & UNIVERSITY ATTENDANCE
Class of 2017 • 442 Students

UNIVERSITY OF CALIFORNIA (66)
Berkeley (15)
Davis (5)
Irvine (6)
Los Angeles (7)
Riverside (3)
San Diego (6)
Santa Barbara (15)
Santa Cruz (33)

CALIFORNIA STATE UNIVERSITY (66)
Cal Poly Pomona (1)
Cal Poly San Luis Obispo (16)
Chico (2)
Fullerton (1)
Humboldt (2)
Monterey Bay (2)
Northridge (4)
San Diego State (9)
San Francisco State (1)
San Jose State (18)
Sonoma (7)

CALIFORNIA - PRIVATE (45)
Azusa Pacific University (2)
Biola University (1)
California College of the Arts (1)
Chapman University (2)
Claremont McKenna College (1)
Columbia College, LA (1)
Concordia University
Harvey Mudd College (1)
Laguna College of Art & Design (1)
Loyola Marymount University (2)
Menlo College (1)
Santa Clara University (5)
Stanford University (3)
University of San Diego (2)
University of Southern California (15)
Westmont College (1)

2-YEAR COLLEGE (65)
Cabrillo College (5)
College of San Mateo (1)
Cuesta College (4)
De Anza College (12)
Feather River College (1)
Foothill College (2)
Lane College (1)
Merritt (1)
Mesa Community College (3)
Mission College (1)
San Francisco City College (1)
San Jose City College (2)
Santa Barbara City College (7)
West Valley College (44)

OUT OF STATE - PRIVATE (66)
Belmont University (1)
Boston College (1)
Boston University (7)
Brown University (2)
Carnegie Mellon University (1)
Carleton College (1)
Colorado Christian University (1)
Cornell University (1)
Dartmouth College (1)
Embry-Riddle University (1)
Fordham University (1)
George Fox University (1)
George Washington University (3)
Gonzaga University (3)
Grinnell College (1)
Hamilton College (1)
Hofstra University (1)
Ithaca College (1)
Johns Hopkins University (2)
Knox College (1)
Lehigh University (1)
LeTourneau University (1)
Marist College (1)
Mount Holyoke College (1)
New York University (4)
Northeastern University (1)
Northwestern University (1)
Oberlin College (1)
Pacific University (1)
Providence College (1)
Reed College (1)
Rice University (2)
Rochester Institute of Technology (1)
Saint Louis University (1)
Seattle University (2)
Southern Methodist University (2)
Stonehill College (1)
Texas Christian University (2)
Tufts University (1)
Tulane University (1)
University of Chicago (1)
University of Denver (1)
University of Notre Dame (1)
University of Pennsylvania (1)
University of Portland (2)
University of Puget Sound (1)
Villanova University (1)
Washington University (1)
Wellesley College (1)
Willamette University (1)
Williams College
Worcester Polytechnic Institute (1)

OUT OF STATE - PUBLIC (78)
Arizona State University (3)
Clemson University (1)
Colorado State University (6)
Colorado School of Mines (2)
George Mason University (1)
Indiana University (1)
Miami of Ohio (1)
MI College of Science & Tech. (1)
Northern Arizona University (1)
Oklahoma State University (1)
Oregon State University (3)
Penn State University (1)
Purdue University (2)
Southern Oregon University (1)
Texas A&M University (1)
United States Naval Academy (1)
University of Alabama (2)
University of Arizona (4)
University of Colorado, Boulder (7)
University of Hawaii (2)
University of Illinois-Champaign-Urbana (4)
University of Iowa (1)
University of Kentucky (1)
University of Michigan (3)
University of Minnesota (2)
University of Nebraska (1)
University of Oregon (18)
University of South Carolina (1)
University of Texas, Austin (2)
University of Washington (6)
University of Wisconsin (1)
University of Wyoming (1)
Virginia Tech University (1)
West Virginia University (1)

INTERNATIONAL COLLEGES (7)
Oxford University (1)
University in Denmark (2)
University of British Columbia (2)
University of Waterloo, Canada (1)
University of Tdu, Finland (1)

OTHER (27)
Gap Year (8)
Travel (2)
Work (14)
Military (3)

CUMULATIVE GRADE POINT DISTRIBUTION
Class of 2018 - Junior Year - 449 Students

- 0.0 - 1.97: 4.5%
- 2.0 - 2.97: 22.5%
- 3.0 - 3.49: 20%
- 3.5 - 3.97: 24%
- 4.0 - 4.72: 29%

POST HIGH SCHOOL PLANS
Class of 2017

- UC: 15%
- CSU: 15%
- CA/PRIVATE: 10%
- OUT OF STATE/PRIVATE: 15%
- OUT OF STATE/PUBLIC: 18%
- 2-YEAR COLLEGE: 19%
- INTERNATIONAL COLLEGES: 2%
- OTHER PLANS: 6%

Los Gatos High School is what I refer to as a "Public-Private," meaning that while it is technically a public school, its location, demographics, and socioeconomic composition offer it the means and resources equivalent to most private schools. According to the real estate database Zillow, the median home value in Los Gatos as of late 2018 was $2 million. By comparison, the median home value in the entire San Jose-Sunnyvale-Santa Clara metropolitan area was $1.2 million. And in East San Jose, where James Lick is located, the median home value was $774,000. [54] And if you are reading this anywhere outside of California, with a perplexed look on your face as you digest those figures, just know that as of 2018 the State of California represented the fifth largest economy in the world according to the U.S. Department of Commerce; with a higher Gross Domestic Product than the entire United Kingdom. [55] It's safe to say that our numbers –and reality– are a bit skewed. But even acknowledging that, there is still a wide range of variance between regionally situated neighborhoods. For a bit of context, the median home value for the entire nation for the same time period was $200,000.

Why bring up this discussion of median home values? Well, as discussed in chapter two, a good portion of the funding for public schools comes from the property taxes of the surrounding area. So it should be quite clear from the exercise above that the average socioeconomic situation of a student at Los Gatos High School is more than likely significantly stronger than that for the average student at James Lick. And as socioeconomic status is closely tied to educational attainment, it is also safe to suspect that the overwhelming majority of Los Gatos students come from a college educated household, and thus have grown up, presumably, in a home environment in which college is the expectation rather than the exception, compulsory rather than exemplary.

A quick review of the Los Gatos school profile will tell you that the enrollment is around 2,040 students. Classes run on an alternating block schedule of 90 minute periods, and that grades are reported on a weighted scale in which "one extra point is given for each ninth through twelfth grade Honors or Advanced Placement course with a C- grade or higher." Los Gatos does not rank its students. As far as curriculum is concerned, Los Gatos offers 18 AP courses and 12 Honors courses. While only 2 years of Math are required for graduation, Los Gatos offers AP Statistics as well as AP Calculus AB and BC.

You may have also noticed that the graduation requirements are essentially identical to James Lick's; the only difference coming in the breakdown of Los Gatos' elective units. However, the college-going rates are substantially different, with seventy-five percent of Los Gatos students heading to four-year schools and nineteen percent heading to two-year schools. You may also notice that there is standardized testing data available for both the SAT and ACT, as well as AP score reporting. Lastly, you will see an exhaustive list of planned college and university attendance for the 442 students in the class of 2017.

There is no demographic or ethnic information provided by the school profile, and unlike the James Lick accompanying Counselor information, Los Gatos does not provide any of this info. But it is a safe assumption that the student body is overwhelmingly Caucasian, with a strong Asian presence, followed by relatively smaller Hispanic / Latino and African-American populations; especially in comparison to surrounding areas.

So what would the average Los Gatos student need to be a competitive applicant for most medium to highly-selective institutions? For me, the consideration of Math preparation is a constant when evaluating applicants. As previously discussed, for anyone with aspirations of a liberal arts or social sciences degree, Statistics, at least, is the preferred math level. Anyone with interests in Business, Engineering, the hard sciences or technology related fields should really be at the Calculus level; and I am always impressed by a student at the Calculus BC level. So again, that remains a constant.

As for a GPA, the Los Gatos school profile actually provides a pie chart detailing the Class of 2018's junior year weighted GPA's. The two largest distributions, 34% and 29%, represent GPA's in the 3.5-3.97 and 4.0-4.72 range, respectively. From my experience, weighted GPA's on a 5 point scale can swing anywhere from .2 to .5 points lower when unweighted. For example, a weighted 3.5 is usually closer to a 3.2 or 3.3 when unweighted. A weighted 4.0 is usually a lot closer to an unweighted 3.6 or 3.7, as students usually take around 2 to 4 AP's in a given year, but can take more. Additionally, for most schools, student's access to AP classes begins junior year. But some schools are AP factories, and students have access as early as the sophomore or even freshman year. With all that in mind, however, what the Los Gatos pie chart tells me is that sixty-three percent (34 plus 29) of the Los Gatos senior class has an unweighted GPA in the 3.2 to 4.0 range, and that sounds about right.

The profile also shows that for the last three academic years, 2015-17, the median SAT score has been around 1180; the median being the middle value in the range of scores. Given that, what I can then deduce is that students in the upper quartile of the class have scores starting in the 1300 and above range. Remember, the max score is a 1600.

So again, generally speaking, if the average student from Los Gatos was able to reach senior year having taken challenging courses, reached a math level of Statistics or higher, achieved at least a 3.3 unweighted cumulative GPA or higher, and scored a 1300 —which correlates to a 27 ACT— or higher on the SAT, then he or she will more than likely have a fighting chance in most medium to highly-selective applicant pools. Especially given the added bonus (for the institutions to which they apply) that the average Los Gatos student more than likely comes from a family with the means to pay the cost of attendance for most public institutions, and probably most private institutions as well.

This financial ability comes into play with Wait List situations, in particular, in which it is the general practice among institutions that very little if any aid will be awarded to students accepted off the Wait List. Additionally, as discussed before, there is a strong correlation to economic standing and test performance; and academic performance, in general. So these are the kinds of students who will more frequently qualify for Merit or academic based scholarships and incentives within given applicant pools. Thus, reducing the overall cost of attendance for a particular institution and increasing their parent's willingness to pay.

Bellarmine College Preparatory (school profile below)

BELLARMINE COLLEGE PREPARATORY

960 WEST HEDDING STREET, SAN JOSE, CA 95126 (408) 294-9224 FAX: (408) 278-1047

CLASS OF 2018 SENIOR PROFILE

History

- **Founded:** 1851
- **Type:** Catholic, Jesuit, Private
- **Enrollment:** 1655
- **Location:** Proximate to Downtown / City Center / Airport
- **Accreditation:** Western Association of Schools & Colleges / Western Catholic Educational Association
- **Membership:** Jesuit Schools Network
  College Board
  National Association for College Admission Counseling
- **Mission:** Bellarmine College Preparatory is a community of men and women gathered together by God for the purpose of educating the student to seek justice and truth throughout his life. We are a Catholic school in the tradition of St. Ignatius of Loyola, the founder of the Society of Jesus. As such, our entire school program is dedicated to forming "men for and with others" - persons whose lives will be dedicated to bringing all their God-given talents to fullness and to living according to the pattern of service inaugurated by Jesus Christ.

Admissions Criteria and Process

- **Eligibility:** Applications are accepted from 8th grade boys enrolled in parochial, independent, and public schools, as well as from qualified transfer applicants in 9th, 10th, and 11th grade.
- **Criteria:** Applicants are evaluated on academic performance in junior high school course work, co-curricular involvement, academic recommendations, results on the High School Placement Test and other standardized tests, and on written essays.

Composition of the Class of 2018: 418 Students

- **Ethnicity:**

African American	4.8%	Filipino/Pacific Islander	7.7%
American Indian	0.2%	Hispanic	16.7%
Asian	11.8%	Indian	7.2%
Caucasian	49.9%	Middle Eastern	1.7%

- **Geographical:** Besides drawing from metropolitan San Jose, students commute from the larger Bay Area. Transportation from distant cities is expedited by the CalTrain stop located adjacent to campus. In the fall of 2017, seniors reside in the following cities:

Campbell	10	Peninsula Cities	26
East Bay	3	San Jose/Santa Clara	243
Los Altos Area	16	South County	21
Los Gatos/Saratoga/Monte Sereno	41	Sunnyvale/Cupertino/Mt. View	28
Fremont/Milpitas/Newark/Union City	30		

Academic Program

- **General:** The academically-talented Bellarmine student follows a curriculum comprised of college preparatory disciplines. Students are required to complete six academic classes in both the Fall and Spring Term. Given the rigor of the standard curriculum students are counseled to limit the number of Honors/AP classes.

- **Curriculum:** Required semesters in traditional liberal arts education: English - 8, Visual/Performing Arts - 3, Mathematics - 6, Modern and Classical Language - 4, Fitness and Health - 2, Science - 6, Social Science - 7, and Religious Studies - 6.

- **Honors/AP Classes:** The Bellarmine philosophy is to provide levels of acceleration and challenge in all sections of a required course and in the elective program. Requesting an Honors/AP course is finalized by the student, with approval of his parents and his counselor, after receiving feedback from his current teacher in that subject area.

- **Honors/AP Sections:** (Available 2017-2018)

Algebra II Honors . . . . 7 Sections	European History AP . . . . 2 Sections	Physics C AP (Mech & E&M) .2 Sections
Biology AP . . . . 2 Sections	Faulkner Seminar Honors . . . . 1 Section	Pre-Calculus Honors . . . . 4 Sections
Calculus AB/AP . . . . 4 Sections	French 4 AP . . . . 1 Section	Statistics AP . . . . 2 Sections
Calculus BC/AP . . . . 3 Sections	Geometry Honors . . . . 3 Sections	Psychology AP . . . . 3 Sections
Chemistry AP . . . . 1 Section	Latin 3 Honors . . . . 1 Section	Spanish 3 Honors . . . . 6 Sections
Chemistry Honors . . . . 5 Sections	AP Latin . . . . 1 Section	Spanish 4 AP . . . . 5 Sections
Computer Science A AP. . . . . .3 Sections	Macroeconomics AP . . . . .4 Sections	Spanish 5 AP . . . . 1 Section
English 1 Honors . . . . 3 Sections	Mandarin 3 Honors . . . . 1 Section	U.S. Gov. & Politics AP . . . . . 5 Sections
English 2 Honors . . . . 3 Sections	Mandarin 4 AP . . . . 1 Section	U.S. History AP. . . . . 3 Sections
English Literature AP. . . . . . . .4 Sections	Multivariable Calculus. . . . . . . 1 Section	World History AP. . . . . 4 Sections
Environmental Science AP . . .8 Sections	Physics 1 AP . . . . .5 Sections	

Testing Statistics

- **PSAT/NMSQT:**

2014	12 Finalists		49 Letters of Commendation
2015	17 Finalists		44 Letters of Commendation
2016	15 Finalists		49 Letters of Commendation
2017	16 Finalists		45 Letters of Commendation
2018		19 Semifinalists	60 Letters of Commendation

- **National Hispanic Scholars:**

2014	14 Scholars	1	Honorable Mention
2015	3 Scholars	2	Honorable Mention
2016	13 Scholars		
2017	7 Scholars		
2018	18 Scholars		

- **Advanced Placement Program:**

	Total Exams	% of 3, 4, 5	2017 Distribution
2014	1364	86%	score of 5...512...34%
2015	1354	83%	score of 4...459...31%
2016	1483	84%	score of 3...308...21%
2017	1485	86%	

College Admission Test Results - Class of 2017: 408 Students

	Median 50%	Mean		
SAT			Biology-E	630
Critical Reading			Biology-M	719
and Writing	590-680	640	Chemistry	701
Math	590-710	650	Literature	661
Total	1180-1400	1300	Math 2	723
ACT			Physics	694
Composite	24-32	28.3	Spanish with Listening	668
			U.S. History	706
			World History	724

Rank-in-Class

- **Grade Point Average:** The school transcript reflects three GPA's. A total GPA includes all grades awarded at Bellarmine. An academic GPA includes all academic course grades awarded. A weighted GPA includes one extra point for each honors or AP grade awarded beginning in the freshman year.

- **Assignment of Rank:** Since the Class of 1994, students have not been ranked. Bellarmine standards for admission are premised on the selection of individuals capable of succeeding in a college preparatory curriculum. Students are admitted selectively and are not retained if they earn less than a 2.0 GPA. The only curricular option is a college preparatory track and 97% enroll in four-year institutions. Since students do not all take the same program, a cumulative ranking system based on raw or weighted grades may not fairly represent a student's relative achievement. A GPA and grade distribution chart accompanies the transcript when sent to college admission offices.

Religious and Guidance Programs

- **Campus Ministry:** The Campus Ministry program supports a Bellarmine student in growing to his fullest self. Through spiritual exploration and honing their gifts to serve as leaders in faith, our students come to better understand how the gifts they have are to be used to make the world more just for all. Our Ignatian values permeate our retreats, Masses, small faith groups, sacraments, and leadership opportunities. Our students leave with a better understanding of what it means to be a servant leader and a person who lives out a faith that serves justice.

- **Christian Service:** The Christian Service program is committed to putting our philosophy of "men for and with others" into action. Our graduation requirement calls for students to complete at least 75 hours working with diverse populations - children, the elderly, the disabled and the socio-economically disadvantaged. Students, faculty, staff, and parents are also involved in annual food, clothing and toy drives, as well as other acts of charity and justice.

- **Guidance:** All juniors take a required two-week course in College Guidance. Individual, personal, and educational counseling is provided for students by professional staff members. Juniors and seniors are assigned to one of the five college counselors for direction in the college decision making process.

- **Religious Studies:** Inspired by the gift of Ignatian spiritual charism, it is the desire that students understand and critically appropriate their own faith tradition in a way that leads to committed action for the sake of the good of others (AMDG). Students take six semesters of Religious Studies to provide a foundation for understanding Scripture as a basis for moral choices and social justice issues.

The Co-Curricular Program (a sampling of over 100 clubs and organizations)

Acts of Kindness	Big Brothers	Indian Student Coalition	Nonsensicals	STEM-MED Club
AGAPE Club	Black Student Union	Italian Heritage Club	Photographic Society	Surfrider Club
Alzheimer's Awareness	Carillon Yearbook	Japan-America	Programming Club	Table Top Games
BCP Ice Hockey	Catholic Gentlemen	Friendship Club	Physics Club	Taekwondo Club
BCP Olympic Lifting	Chinese Culture Club	KBCP Radio	Quiz Bowl	The Bell Online
BCP Roller Hockey	Cinema Club	Korean Club	Robotics Team	Theatre Tech
BCP Rugby	Cooking Club	Latino Student Union	Sandwich Service Club	Ultimate Frisbee
Beach Volleyball	Cycling Club	Makerspace	Sanguine Humours	Vietnamese Student
Bellarmine Armed	Filipino Student Assoc.	Math Club	Science Bowl	Union
Forces Club	Fishing Club	Model U.N. Club	SEAS (Student Environmental	We Share Solar
Bellarmine Political	Futsal Club	Muslim Student	Action Society)	Writer's Guild
Review	Gay Straight Community	Awareness Club	Ski Club	Yell Leaders

- **Drama:** Bellarmine Theatre Arts features three shows per season, along with two year-round improvisational comedy troupes. Over 120 students work annually in performance, stagecraft, and production of shows. 2016-2017 productions included *Peter and the Starcatcher*, *Pippin* and *The Coward*. Our state-of-the-art, 400-seat Main Stage Theatre and its adjoining Black Box Theatre opened in 2010.

- **Speech and Debate:** Over 100 students participate in the Speech and Debate program. Bellarmine has won the state speech and debate championships 12 of the last 16 years. We typically send twenty or more students to the state tournament. In the past 15 years, 73 students have won individual state championships. In the last 15 years, Bellarmine has ten national champions and 41 national finalists.

- **Interscholastic Athletics:** Baseball (3 levels), Basketball (4), Cross Country (4), Football (3), Golf (2), Lacrosse (2), Soccer (3), Swimming (2), Tennis (2), Track (2), Water Polo (3), Wrestling (3), Volleyball (3).

- **Central Coast Section CCS Championships Division 1**

Football	1981, 1986, 1990, 2008, 2009, 2011, 2015
Baseball	1985, 1986, 1987, 1988, 1999, 2006
Basketball	1993, 1995, 1996, 1999, 2003, 2004, 2008, 2009, 2010, 2012, 2013, 2014, 2015
Swimming	2004, 2005, 2006, 2007, 2008, 2009, 2010, 2011, 2012, 2013, 2014, 2015, 2017
Tennis	1982, 1983, 1986, 1988, 1989
Water Polo	1999, 2000, 2001, 2002, 2003, 2004, 2005, 2006, 2009, 2011, 2012, 2013, 2016
Cross Country	1993, 1994, 1995, 1996, 1997, 1998, 1999, 2000, 2011, 2013, 2014, 2015, 2016
Golf	1986, 1995, 1996, 2004, 2005, 2015, 2016
Soccer	1994, 1995, 1997, 1999, 2000, 2001, 2002, 2005, 2008, 2009, 2011, 2014, 2015
Track	1990, 1994, 2000, 2001, 2002, 2007, 2010, 2013, 2015, 2016, 2017
Volleyball	1998, 1999, 2000, 2001, 2003, 2005, 2007, 2008, 2009, 2010, 2011, 2016
Wrestling	2001

Bellarmine Graduates of 2017 are Attending

Percentage attending College in Fall of 2017 .... 99.3%
Percentage attending a Four Year Institution 96.6%
Percentage attending a Two Year Institution 3.2%
Percentage attending a School Out-of-State 47.5%

- **University of California**

Berkeley	14
Davis	1
Irvine	4
Los Angeles	5
Merced	1
Riverside	1
San Diego	8
Santa Barbara	6
Santa Cruz	9

- **California State University**

California Polytechnic SLO	21
East Bay	2
Fullerton	1
Sacramento	1
San Diego	2
San Francisco	2
San Jose	6
Sonoma	1
Stanislaus	1

- **Jesuit Colleges & Universities**

Boston College	5
Creighton University	4
Fordham University	4
Georgetown University	6
Gonzaga University	7
Loyola Marymount University	19
Loyola University Chicago	2
Regis University	1
Saint Louis University	2
Santa Clara University	37
Seattle University	8
University of San Francisco	7
Xavier University	3

- **Private Schools in California**

California College of the Arts (San Francisco)	1
Chapman University	6
Harvey Mudd College	1
John Paul the Great Catholic University	1
Menlo College	1
Pepperdine University	1
Saint Mary's College of California	3
Stanford University	3

University of Redlands	9
University of San Diego	9
University of Southern California	11
University of the Pacific	1

- **Out of State Schools**

American University	1
Arizona State University	2
Baylor University	1
Benedictine College	1
Boise State University	5
Boston University	2
Bowling Green State University	1
Bucknell University	1
Carnegie Mellon University	2
Colgate University	1
Colorado State University	6
Columbia University	1
DePaul University	2
Emory University	1
Embry-Riddle Aeronautical University	1
Georgia Institute of Technology	1
Idaho State University	1
Juniata College	1
Lindenwood University	1
Linfield College	1
Massachusetts Institute of Technology	4
Michigan State University	2
Montana State University, Bozeman	1
Northeastern University	5
Northern Arizona University	2
Oregon State University	8
Pacific University	1
Pennsylvania State University	2
Purdue University	6
Rochester Institute of Technology	1
Saint Anselm College	1
Saint Michael's College	1
Seton Hall University	1
Southern Methodist University	3
St. John's University, Queens Campus	1
Swarthmore College	1
Texas Christian University	3
The Catholic University of America	1

The George Washington University	1
The Ohio State University	1
The University of Alabama	2
The University of Arizona	5
The University of Texas, Arlington	1
The University of Texas, Austin	2
Trinity University	1
University of Chicago	2
University of Colorado, Boulder	4
University of Maine	1
University of Miami	1
University of Michigan	2
University of Minnesota, Twin Cities	1
University of Missouri, Columbia	1
University of Nevada, Reno	13
University of Notre Dame	4
University of Oregon	5
University of Portland	6
University of Puget Sound	1
University of Tennessee, Knoxville	2
University of Virginia	1
University of Washington	1
Virginia Tech	1
Wake Forest University	2
Washington University in St. Louis	1
Weber State University	1
Western Oregon University	1
Western Washington University	1
Whitman College	1
Whittier College	1
Willamette University	1
Worcester Polytechnic Institute	1

- **Military Academies**

U.S. Air Force Academy	1
U.S. Military Academy - Army	2
U.S. Naval Academy	1

- **International Schools**

ETH Zurich	1
University of Edinburgh	1
University of Toronto	1
University of Waterloo	1

- **Community Colleges** — 13
- **Other Plans** — 1

PRESIDENT	PRINCIPAL	DIRECTOR OF ADMISSIONS	COLLEGE COUNSELORS	
Chris Meyercord '88	Kristina Luscher	Joe Wagstaffe '91	Mary Connolly	Katy Murphy, Director
			Jack Doyle	Ed Schoenberg
			Chris Fleitas	

A quick look at the three school profiles "side by side" and one can immediately notice a distinct difference in resources for the three schools. As where James Lick's profile is a single page, Los Gatos' is two pages, and Bellarmine's is four. The Bellarmine profile touches on its history –one of the oldest high schools in the state– the fact that it is an all-boys school, and is founded in the Jesuit tradition. It also explicitly lays out, on the first page, the ethnic and geographic breakdown of the senior class.

As for the curriculum at Bellarmine, three years of Mathematics are required for graduation, but again, there are several sections of AP Calculus BC offered; with 22 AP's offered in total, and 11 Honors courses, with no limits on the amount students can take. Bellarmine has weighted GPA's, but has not ranked students since the mid-1990's. There is information on the co-curricular programs offered, such as social and cultural clubs, speech and debate, as well as a long and storied history of athletic program successes. Also, just like Los Gatos, there is an exhaustive listing of the colleges and universities attended by the year's previous class.

What one might have missed when looking at the profile, but is of significant import, is that "all juniors take a required two-week course in College Guidance." Additionally, each of the juniors and seniors are assigned to one of five college counselors for assistance in the college search and decision-making process. Therein lies the resources of a private school; and it is to the detriment and fault of the student and family that does not take advantage of such resources, especially when they're paying for it. This helps to explain the school's ninety-seven percent four-year college going rate.

Academically, a good percentage of the Bellarmine boys are high fliers; although not all. In the testing section of the profile you will see that for the past four years Bellarmine has produced an average of fifteen National Merit Scholar Finalists, an average of eleven National Hispanic Scholars over the past five years, and that for the past four years, of the 1,424 AP tests taken annually by Bellarmine boys, an average of eighty-five percent of those tests have received scores of 3, 4, or 5. The mean SAT and ACT scores for the Class of 2017 were 1300 and 28.3, respectively. An additional GPA Distribution —as of May 2017— sheet provided with the profile, for the Class of 2018, indicates that nearly sixty-two percent of the 418 (then) juniors had cumulative weighted GPA's in the 3.6 and above range. Again, given the average .2-.3% drop when unweighted, that would equate to more than half of the senior class having an unweighted GPA of about 3.3 or 3.4 and above; very similar to Los Gatos.

So in the end, a Bellarmine student looking to make himself a competitive applicant at most mid to highly-selective institutions, would plan for an academic schedule and aim for academic numbers very similar to that of a Los Gatos student aiming for the same goal: a Math level of at least Statistics or higher, a GPA of 3.3 or above, and a 1300 SAT or 28 ACT. In contrast to Los Gatos though, that 1300 SAT and 28 ACT represent the mean, or average, test scores for Bellarmine boys, and represent scores in the top quartile of Los Gatos students; meaning there are a good number of Bellarmine students with scores of 1400 and 30 or higher on the SAT and ACT, respectively. Additionally, one important piece to note here is that, as was stated above, Bellarmine has a ninety-seven percent four-year college-going rate. Thus, while thirty-eight percent of the class had GPA's under an unweighted 3.3, all but a handful of them, percentage-wise, still got into four-year colleges. A prime example of the difference in resources at play for the different high schools, and their respective families' abilities to pay for college.

Summary

It's important to recognize that we've discussed the characteristics that would make for competitive applicants in very general terms. At no point was race, ethnicity, or gender mentioned, although Bellarmine is an all-boys school.

Additionally, I've chosen to focus solely on academic criteria as there is no "one-size fits all" description of what a compelling personal side looks like in a holistic admission review. My best advice there is to get involved in the extra-curricular activities that interest you, and to not be boring in your essay or application.

I've focused on competitiveness for medium to highly-selective institutions for a reason, as public school systems in most states, if not all, readily provide admission criteria on their websites and printed materials. Admission criteria for mid to highly-selective schools can be, and in reality has to be, a bit more nebulous in nature, and therefore it is always best to speak in general terms when discussing the probability of admission. Let this serve as another reminder that no counselor –independent or otherwise– should ever guarantee admission to a particular school for a particular student. Even public schools must contend with impaction and overcrowded campuses, meaning some, or many, qualified applicants will be turned away from year to year.

So while students should always strive to achieve the strongest numbers possible, what I've attempted to do is simply contextualize what would make for competitive applicants from each of the different types of high schools discussed. And do not focus solely on the sample schools provided. Those three were chosen as proxies for schools in their respective categories, as I've designated them. I have traveled the country and visited high schools in towns and cities all across the land. Nearly every major metropolitan area in the country has a similarly representative set of high schools.

Conversely, and this is an important point to make, a particular student does not have a better chance of attending a particular type of college or university based *solely* on the type of high school they attend. Students must apply themselves, regardless of the environment they find themselves in. From our perch as Admission Officers it is actually quite apparent when a student has attended a school with numerous resources, and for whatever reason, has made use of virtually none of them. Those decisions are pretty easy to make, by the way.

In reality, what this exercise clearly illustrates is the fact that differences in resources can and do lead to differences in outcomes. More resources equal more opportunities, and more opportunities lead to more and varied options. Along those lines, it is fundamental to this conversation to recognize the role of socioeconomics in college attainment. Usually, the higher up the socioeconomic ladder you go, the stronger the attachment and commitment to educational attainment at both the parent and student level; one the obvious by-product of the other.

This exercise goes to the heart of the very reason for this book. My intent has been to illustrate that college admission, or the process of getting into college, is not, in fact, rocket science. I know the stress that students and families feel when approaching senior year. I encounter it on a daily basis. I know that students, families, and counselors talk this stuff up to such a feverish pitch that no one knows how anyone will be accepted into school X, Y, or Z. Somehow folks actually begin to believe that certain schools only accept 4.0 GPA and 1600 SAT caliber students when the reality is that the national average for the ACT is a 20, which equates to about a 1030-1050 on the SAT, and the national average admit rate for all colleges and universities in 2016 was 65.4% percent [56]; it was 66.1% percent in 2015. Only twenty percent (19.5%) of all colleges and universities have an admit rate lower than fifty percent! [57] Point being, most students have many more college options than they realize. Or at least they could if only they widened their pool of potential schools.

To that end, I realize that a good amount of the anxiety surrounding college admission is not centered on whether or not students will get into *any* college, but rather a particular college; usually that student's, or parent's, more often than not, dream or *stretch* school. In those instances I can only offer that it is important to be realistic in this process. Often times students, parents, counselors, and even universities themselves, can get all too wrapped in *Keeping up with the Joneses*; in chasing a name or a brand, some prestige or recognition they feel deserving of, when in reality they would be much better suited and served in a different environment altogether.

I do my best to diffuse these stresses, both self-imposed and genuine, for those families I am lucky enough to interact with. But in the bigger picture I know that those interactions are only a drop in the bucket. And so I write this with the intent that any student, any parent, or any counselor from any high school in the country can pick this book up and begin to realize that there is a lot more in their control than they realize. I write this for the benefit of the student: any student and all students. I write this to empower the overworked public school counselor whose caseload is, on average, close to 500 students. I write this for the AVID (Advancement Via Individual Determination) teacher, or any teacher attempting to guide a pupil in this process. I write it for the stressed out parent who feels lost at sea, stranded, and without a clue where to begin; for the parent who feels pressured to hire an educational consultant, or as though they've cheated their student if they do not. I write it for colleagues who will hopefully find solidarity in my words, and some sense of relief that alas, the obvious has been stated.

Hopefully those who read this will see that there is essentially a pattern to competitiveness for students at any given school: a competitive grade point average, math preparation, overall schedule rigor, and scores within the top third to twenty percent of the class, all in addition to being an interesting person. A student who can excel in those areas, regardless of geographic location, financial situation, race, ethnicity, or parental education level, will undoubtedly put him or herself in a desirable position in the eyes of most colleges and universities. It's not rocket science, folks.

Chapter 5

Tying It All Together

OK class, pop quiz time. What have we learned so far?

Well, for starters, we talked about demographics and socioeconomics; *because it's always important to know the numbers*. We started by offering a visual "lay of the land," as it were, and explaining just how many of us there are all together as a nation, and of certain racial or ethnic groups individually. And that's important information to know period, but also because it helps to give one a realistic frame of reference in discussions of access, resources, and equity. It helps to solidify the concept of diversity. It helps to explain why certain parts of the country lack it and why colleges and universities are in constant search of it.

We talked about the correlation between educational attainment and socioeconomic advancement. Remember the equation?

Education + Time = $$

Good. You remembered. It's simple, right? We demonstrated the gradual increase in wealth and quality of life, generally speaking, the higher the level of the degree attained. Remember the poverty statistics correlated to educational attainment? Did the poverty rate increase or decrease the higher the level of education? That's right, it decreased. Pretty straightforward.

Up next we covered what, to some, may have sounded a bit like environmental determinism; essentially, the theory that one's environment and surroundings will ultimately decide their level of success in the world. And I want to be clear, dear reader, that that is not what we discussed. What we deliberated was the impact of discriminatory federal and state residential policies —*the effects of which have never truly been addressed or corrected*— which have helped create the de facto segregation we currently see in our K-12 education nationwide. Those historical realities have shaped present day outcomes which only persist in maintaining the status quo; of sustaining the Achievement Gap, educationally and ultimately socioeconomically. If we were clear before then let's be crystal now, the system is not designed for everyone to succeed. There must be a lower if there is to be a middle and upper. But fear not, dear pupil, because the key to your advancement rests in your hands: your education. As I stated in the beginning of our time together, education is elevation: out of poverty, out of ignorance, out of oppression. And therein lies its power. The truly impressive among you will find ways to harness that power through whatever obstacles come their way.

Next we talked about your options in achieving your education. We talked about big research universities, small liberal arts colleges, and the medium-sized comprehensive schools in between. Remember, no one school is a perfect fit for all. Do your research, know your options, and visit as many schools as you can. Remember that community colleges are there for a purpose, and that purpose is both more useful and more utilized than many realize or will acknowledge. Use the community college for what it was intended to be: a stepping-stone to your four-year degree or a specialized certification.

You'll recall the Case Study exercise in which we looked at three San Jose, California high schools: a public, a public-private, and a private school. We examined the school profiles for each and discussed what a student would need to accomplish at each in order to make him or herself a viable candidate for admission to a medium to highly-selective college or university. You'll notice, hopefully, that we never broached the subject of a particular applicant's race or ethnicity in the case study. And I hope you realized at the end that we didn't actually need to for the purposes of our discussion; although I am most definitely a proponent of doing so in real life, and in actual admission considerations. There is only so much that a high school student is in control of: what they do in school and how well they do it. The other stuff, who they are, where they were born, how rich or poor their parents are, etc., is out of their control. And so they should not be rewarded or penalized for such things in the college admission process. But context, including the consideration of race or ethnicity, is always helpful. And if nothing else, Admission Counselors should be encouraged to make decisions that make sense within the context of a given applicant pool.

The bottom line, though, and what perhaps should have been the main take-away from that exercise, is that resources matter. Admission professionals see this all the time. As where it's easy to make the generalization that poorer students from poorer schools tend to perform more poorly, it's also apt to imply that wealthy families simply have the means and resources to get poor performance diagnosed and explained away. And they do so quite frequently. Resources can have all the impact in the world with regard to a student's opportunities, or their chances to take advantage of any opportunities that come their way. Richer students are not inherently smarter students by virtue of their wealth. They simply tend to perform better as they deal less directly and less frequently with life's major obstacles, in addition to being surrounded by more examples of success. So again, just to drill it home, know that resources matter.

One thing we haven't touched on much, which I promised we would, is cost. And let me start by admitting that this is, to me, a real area of concern for the entire Higher Education industry. We are at a point where a serious stratification of access is taking shape, with several private colleges and universities nearing an $80,000 a year total cost of attendance. Eighty thousand dollars: annually! That's a $320,000 undergraduate education, which is, quite frankly, ridiculous and unsustainable. And there is no sign of costs somehow slowing or magically decreasing any time soon. In the next fifteen to twenty years I honestly wouldn't be surprised to see a $100,000 a year Cost of Attendance at a top-tier institution. It would be a disappointing development, for sure, but not a surprising one. And again, it makes no sense in a logical world. Not when the average starting salary for a college graduate is in the neighborhood of $50,000. [58]

The average cost of tuition, fees, and room and board at public universities in the 2018-19 academic year was $29,400, accounting for both in-state and out-of-state students. It was $48,500 for private non-profit four years. And while the public school option is clearly the most affordable of the two, there's something to the saying "you get what you pay for." Because while the national (six-year) graduation rate is fifty-eight percent overall, it's seventy-six percent for four-year private nonprofits, sixty-six percent for four-year publics, and only 37.3% for private for-profit four-year colleges. [59] That is to say that while private schools may cost more, the reality is that more and more these days, it's taking longer to complete a Bachelor's degree at most of the nation's public schools. Thus, the costs may come closer to evening out than you think.

In terms of paying for school, there are options. The first option, and perhaps the one most in the student's control, is to be a strong student. Merit based or academic scholarships are offered at nearly every school in the nation; several of the Ivies do not offer merit, however, and instead utilize need-based aid. Just by virtue of being a good student with a strong GPA, a rigorous course load, and scores in the top twenty percent of a respective college or university's applicant pool, a student could potentially receive anywhere from a few thousand dollars a year to a full-ride. How's that for motivation?

Option two would be need-based aid offered by the respective university: a combination of scholarships, grants, work-study options, and loans. And in order to qualify for such funds there are forms which must be filled out and submitted, *in a timely fashion*. The FAFSA, which stands for the Free Application for Federal Student Aid, is a required document at most institutions throughout the country. The College Scholarship Service Profile, or the CSS Profile, is an additional form required at most private institutions; there is a nominal fee for the profile in relation to the potential thousands it could qualify an applicant for. As I tell students and families all the time, regardless of whether or not you think you are going to qualify for need-based aid it makes sense to put yourself in the best position possible by filing and submitting the forms. Year after year, without fail, decisions go out and families call asking for more money. But when I ask whether or not they submitted the forms they respond with "Well, we didn't think we would qualify." And so you didn't even try? That simply doesn't make sense to me. Personally, I would want to know for certain one way or the other.

The third option would be outside scholarships accumulated by the student and used to pay for college. Literally, as I was typing this sentence, I Googled "Starbucks scholarships," [60] "McDonald's scholarships," [61] and "Target Scholarships," [62] and guess what I found, actual sites for each of those companies dedicated to helping students pay for college. There are numerous web sites that compile scholarships, and it's a reality that every year large sums of money designated for such scholarships goes unused as students never bother to apply. There are scholarships for a wide range of categories and student characteristics. Some are nominal. Some are substantial. But as the cliché goes, any little bit helps. Most of these scholarships require an essay from the applicant. So in reality, once you've crafted an essay for one, there are probably only minor edits needed to tailor it for another. The research into these scholarships should begin sophomore year, with earnest effort in the junior year, so that you're ready to meet deadlines in senior year. All too often families come to our offices asking for additional scholarships at the point of admission. That's simply too late. Do the homework early and come to the table prepared.

Lastly, in the discussion of paying for college we must broach the subject of loans. Loans are a reality of higher education, plain and simple. For most college-going students, unless you are lucky enough to receive a full-ride academic or athletic scholarship, loans will comprise at least some portion of your financial aid. As where scholarships and grants are "free money," loans, by definition, you must pay back. There are student loans, parent loans, federally subsidized and unsubsidized loans, etc.; at least, those are the only types of loans I would ever recommend considering. Whenever you hear the term "private loan" you should stop immediately, and evaluate your situation. Here is where one must be smart in their approach. Far too often, we as Admission Counselors, or Financial Aid officers, must coax students and families down from the ledge of financial insolvency. Sometimes a school you've been admitted to simply is not a financial reality. Hopefully, you've done your research and applied to a reasonable range of institutions which have in turn yielded some reasonable financial options. If you have aspirations of graduate school, and I would hope that you do, you must attempt, as best you can, to factor those costs into your plan as well. Be reasonable. Don't bite off more than you can chew.

The last bit of advice I will leave you with is this: the Internet is forever. To all the youngsters out there intent on sharing your every waking thought with the world through social media, just know that when you are young you do and say stupid things. That is the immaturity inherent in youth, and occasionally even in adulthood. Do you really want those momentary lapses in judgment immortalized in a tweet, an Instagram post, a Snapchat or viral Facebook rant? Think before you post. Or better yet, just don't post. There is a good chance that thirty year old you won't necessarily agree with the worldview of fifteen, eighteen, or even twenty-three year old you. It's called growth. It's a good thing. Don't let your young-self keep your adult-self from being gainfully employed someday, or your seventeen year old self from being admitted to the school of your dreams. And that ain't rocket science, folks. That's just being smart.

A Pause for Sanity:

Admission Not Guaranteed

In March of 2019 news broke of a college admission scandal involving an educational consultant and wealthy families, in which the consultant, William Rick Singer, coordinated the bribery of coaches, administrators, and test proctors to ensure students' entry into some of the nation's most elite campuses. The FBI operation, known as "Varsity Blues," would charge more than fifty individuals in six states, including high-powered corporate executives, and Hollywood actors. Not one Admission official at any of the institutions involved was charged or implicated in the initial disclosure of the investigation, yet the case still resonated as an *Admission* scandal; as it rightly should have. The perpetrators did what they did to gain access to the respective institutions. In a sense, we in the Admission field, or at least the uber competitive, hyper-selective faction of us, created the desire for Mr. Singer's services, even if we were unaware of the actions being taken. We were culturally culpable even if we were factually ignorant.

And while the news was shocking to some, as we learned of the depths of deceit and criminality to which some of the actors involved sank to, in the bigger picture it was a lot less so. This was simply another example of the role of resources in relation to access: rich people were willing to buy their child's way into the college of their choice, *sometimes* completely unbeknownst to the students themselves. That alone is a social and cultural conversation worthy of its own book. But that, alone, is not as alarming a trend to me as it may be to others. The bad actors were caught, eventually. Any potential additional offenders have been put on notice. There may be more scrutiny in athletic recruitment and development fund-raising, and perhaps even some regulation of Independent Counselors and Educational Consultants in the works. The scandal happened, and it may well quickly be forgotten; especially given the nature of our 24/7 news cycle and the perpetual search for the next big story. More alarming to me, however, is the developing situation in which a failed Texas politician has been gaining momentum in his quest to eradicate –completely– the consideration of race, and all its varied implications, in college admission; also known as Affirmative Action.

I often find that when folks from a given majority (of any country, really) make claims of inequality or discrimination being shown towards them, what they are actually calling for is the maintenance or heightening of the status quo; attempting to increase the systemic and institutionalized discrimination and inequality already in place and geared towards minorities. It is reverse psychology: the victimizer claiming victimization. The coffee calling the kettle black, figuratively –and sometimes literally– speaking. In such a socially and politically polarized environment as the country currently finds itself in, racing towards 2020, it seems it is *He* who screams the loudest who shall have the last word, regardless of the *nonsense* He may be spewing. And that is essentially the situation we face with the series of lawsuits brought against The University of Texas, The University of North Carolina, and Harvard University. Each case designed and intended to reach the halls of the Supreme Court, each case claiming that the consideration of race was used to the detriment of the plaintiff, and each orchestrated by the disingenuously named *Students for Fair Admissions*; a group coordinated and masterfully puppeteered by a financial advisor and unsuccessful Texas Congressional candidate, named Edward Blum.

As a 2017 New York Times article explained, "Mr. Blum has orchestrated more than two dozen lawsuits challenging affirmative action practices and voting rights laws across the country." [63] He lost the University of Texas case, but won his case against the Voting Rights Act of 1965, effectively paving the way for the rampant voter suppression currently taking place (*as in, during the 2018 mid-terms*) in several southern states. As the author put it, the key accomplishment of Mr. Bloom has been his ability to bring together Conservative donors, high-powered Republican establishment lawyers, and "students and others who believe they are being mistreated in the name of racial justice." [64]

And in all fairness, this is a tricky topic. Especially for those who tend to shy away from discussions of race and inequality, either out of genuine discomfort or intentional ignorance. But the reality is that Mr. Bloom's efforts and intentions are all too clearly transparent to anyone attuned to the realities of our history as a country and life in the present day. As was stated in chapter one, the term minority isn't merely a descriptor for non-white Americans. It is a physical, social, and economic reality. There are quantifiably less folks of various ethnic groups (1) in the country as a whole, (2) in schools at the K-12 level and in higher education in general, (3) in certain sectors of the workforce, particularly in professions such as medicine, law, and STEM related fields, (4) in the higher rungs of the socioeconomic ladder, and (5) in politics. And there are many real and significant social, political, historical, media and criminal justice system related factors behind those realities; an example of which we saw in chapter two with the discriminatory FHA regulations. So any attempts to dismantle the very recent – *as in, within the last 50 years*– legal and societal measures aimed at addressing and remedying these realities, all in the name of "fairness and equity," are either misguided or outright contemptuous. And in this case I think it's safe to assume the latter.

Mr. Bloom's involvement in the Harvard case is especially spurious, as he has attempted to harness the misguided plight of a true minority in his efforts to pursue what equates to a White Nationalist agenda: the complete erasure of racial or ethnic consideration in university admission, a result that would only serve to increase the widening educational attainment gap. Now of the three suits brought by Students for Fair Admissions, the Harvard case is the most qualified and interesting, as the filing claims that "Harvard's Affirmative Action policies" effectively create a quota system which disadvantages qualified Asian applicants.

To be clear, Harvard is the oldest and one of the most selective institutions in the country. The admit rate at Harvard, like many of the Ivy League schools, has been in the single digits for many many years; as in upwards of ninety percent of the applicants to these schools are denied year after year. For the fall of 2018, Harvard's admit rate was less than five percent; only slightly higher than Stanford University's, which has been the lowest in the country for several years now. So low, in fact, that they have decided to stop publishing it altogether in an admirable –albeit too late– attempt, I think, to lessen the angst of their applicants. The point being, and the major take away for anybody interested in this story, is that admission criteria for highly-selective schools is, and by definition must be, a bit nebulous and arbitrary. These schools receive far too many statistically qualified applicants than they could ever hope to admit. So factors outside of perfect test scores and GPA's must and do come into play.

And this is where *the rub* comes for the Asian plaintiffs. Because as Harvard was forced to uncover some of its admission practices during the course of the case —an outcome which surely pleased Mr. Blum and his confederates— it was discovered that Asian applicants routinely received less than stellar ratings for their personal attributes, with Admission reviewers even going so far as to coin a melancholy phrase for the average Asian applicant. And while I am not familiar with the inner-workings of Harvard's selection process, nor do I agree with the terminology used, as a seasoned Admission professional I genuinely understand where the university is coming from.

One difficult part of the Harvard conversation that most shy away from, in large part due to the discomfort that racial or ethnically charged topics induce in general, is that is the Asian demographic is, generally speaking, (1) a small but powerful socioeconomic contingent of the population, (2) a community with an unmatched and unwavering dedication to academic excellence, but also, and this is key to the discussion, (3) a very status-driven culture as a whole. Meaning that, with respect to higher education, many Asian students and families seek out, apply to, and expect to be admitted to only the highest ranked and most well-regarded institutions throughout the country. The former *Daily Show* contributor, comic, and social commentator, Hassan Manaj, referenced this with his "Stanford or bust" analogy of the exchanges he shared with his father throughout his childhood. It's the essence of what Author Amy Chua characterized as a "strict Chinese upbringing" in her wildly popular book *Battle Hymn of the Tiger Mother*. [65] It's the overriding parental and cultural stressor that many second and third generation Asian-American applicants write about in their college essays.

The Asian demographic makes up only six percent of the American population, yet they comprise, by far, the largest ethnic minority presence at most of the nation's elite campuses:

Percentage of Asian Students in the entering Freshman Class

UC Berkeley (Fall 2018) - 42% [66]
UCLA (Fall 2017) - 28% [67]
Stanford (Fall 2017) - 22% [68]
USC (Fall 2018) - 17% [69]
Michigan (Fall 2018) - 15% [70]
Harvard (Fall 2018) - 23% [71]

And that's not even counting the international student population on those campuses, which tends to be highly concentrated with Chinese and Indian students; USC's international student population for the Fall 2018 class was 24%. A part of the question then becomes, "How much representation is over-representation?" As a veteran Admission professional, I can tell you that there is a familiar staccato to the high-flying Asian applicant. Additionally, I can tell you that not all Asian students are high-flyers academically, but that statistically as a group, they are without question the strongest, on average. For those strong students though, of course the academics will be there: the GPA near the top of the class, the scores well above average or nearly perfect, the course rigor strong, comprised of the most challenging courses the high school can offer. And on the personal side, there will more than likely be a musical instrument mastered since childhood for the Chinese or Korean applicant, participation in the cultural dance Bharatanatyam for the Indian female applicant, Badminton, membership in the Robotics, Chess, or Math clubs of a given school, etc. And in terms of the chosen or intended majors of most Asian applicants, there is a short list of desired and culturally approved paths: usually STEM fields or business related. It's almost formulaic. In being so, I can understand the Harvard reviewer's general malaise with the average –more than likely well above average– Asian applicant they must see. That said, I can almost guarantee that these traits are never used against the Asian applicant in the Harvard admission review; or in any other university's admission review for that matter. It simply becomes typical of the package presented; exceptionalism becomes average.

And again, there is nothing wrong with this reality. There is nothing wrong with the fact that Asian students aim for top-tier institutions and the highest paying majors at a disproportionate rate when compared to their peers. Nothing wrong with cultural appreciation and participation throughout the high school years. And absolutely nothing wrong with complete and total dedication to academic superiority, above all else but family. But there is something wrong with perspective being skewed to the point that, as an applicant, you don't realize that you are part of a bigger picture. You are one of however many hundreds or thousands of students that a particular institution will be considering for entry into its hallowed grounds and storied traditions. You are a part of a mosaic that is much grander than the skillfully crafted self-portrait you've painted over the last eighteen years. You are an applicant to a university, and you are *not* guaranteed admission simply because you think you are; because you check off all the boxes of the assumed admission criteria you've crafted in your mind for school X, Y, or Z.

If you're a young white woman with a subpar GPA and less than stellar test scores, you are not being denied admission to the University of Texas because some undeserving minority *stole* your spot. You simply weren't as competitive as you needed to be, especially given the fact that the University of Texas is over forty percent Caucasian. It would be more apt to make the argument that you weren't as competitive as the rest of the forty percent of the class that you ethnically resembled. If you're an Asian student with a perfect GPA and perfect scores and you didn't get into Harvard, you simply didn't get into Harvard; just like the rest of other ninety percent of Harvard's applicants, a good proportion of which had a very similar academic profile. If you are an African-American or Hispanic student on an Ivy League campus, or any campus for that matter, know that you didn't steal that spot by virtue of your skin color. You earned that spot by virtue of the hard work you put in, just like your peers. Race or ethnicity *alone* will never determine an admission decision. Period. Admission professionals must weigh a myriad array of factors when comprising a class. And given the potential implications that the social construct of race can have on one's life experience, as evidenced throughout history on to today, race and ethnicity should be one of those factors; never the only one, but definitely one of the many.

The point is, admission to any particular school is not certain, it is not guaranteed, and it is most definitely not owed to you. Neither is a certain scholarship or financial aid package, a certain dorm style or roommate, a spot on the team, a parking space, professor or class time, etc. Pursuing a higher education in this country is a privilege, not a right. You need to earn it; *not conspire to lie, cheat, and pay for it.* And in the end you need to be OK with things not going exactly as you wanted or planned. Because I have news for you, that's how life works sometimes.

THE END

Bibliography

Intro

1) P.14 Clinedinst, Melissa, and Anna-Maria

   Koranteng. *2017 State of College Admission*. NACAC,

   2018, pp. 1–40, *2017 State of College Admission*.

Chapter 1

2) P.17 US Census Bureau. "Monthly Population Estimates

   for the United States: April 1, 2010 to December 1,

   2019." United States Census Bureau. Feb. 2019.

   https://www.census.gov/data/datasets/time-

   series/demo/popest/2010s-national-

   total.html#par_textimage_1810472256.

3) P. 18 Data Access and Dissemination Systems (DADS).

   "American FactFinder - Results." American FactFinder -

   Results. 05 Oct. 2010. Unites States Census Bureau. 20

Dec. 2018.

<https://factfinder.census.gov/bkmk/table/1.0/en/ACS/1

7_5YR/DP05/0100000US>.

4) P.18 US Census Bureau. "Educational Attainment in the

United States: 2017." Educational Attainment in the

United States: 2017. 11 Dec. 2017. Unites States Census

Bureau. 6 Dec. 2018

<https://census.gov/data/tables/2017/demo/education-

attainment/cps-detailed-tables.html>.

5) P.19 US Census Bureau. "High School Completion Rate Is

Highest in U.S. History." The United States Census

Bureau. 19 Mar. 2018. Unites States Census Bureau. 2

Jan. 2019 <https://census.gov/newsroom/press-

releases/2017/educational-attainment-2017.html>.

6) P.20 See 5.

7) P.20 See 3.

8) P. 20 See 4.

9) P. 22 "Front Page." *Social Science Data Analysis Network*

   /, www.ssdan.net/.

10) P. 23 "Demographic Maps: Non-Hispanic White

    Population." *CensusScope*, Social Science Data Analysis

    Network, www.censusscope.org/us/map_nhwhite.html.

11) P. 24 United States, Census Bureau, Population Division.

    "Current Population Survey: 2017 Annual Social and

    Economic Supplement." Cited December 6, 2018.

12) P. 25 "Demographic Maps: Hispanic

    Population." *CensusScope*, Social Science Data Analysis

    Network, 2000,

    www.censusscope.org/us/map_hispanicpop.html.

13) P. 25 "Demographic Maps: African-American

    Population." *CensusScope*, Social Science Data Analysis

    Network, 2000,

    www.censusscope.org/us/map_nhblack.html.

14) P. 26 "Demographic Maps: Asian

    Population." *CensusScope*, Social Science Data Analysis

Network, 2000,

www.censusscope.org/us/map_nhasian.html.

15) P.26 Chappell, Bill. "Census Finds A More Diverse

America, As Whites Lag Growth." NPR. 22 June 2017.

NPR. 18 Dec. 2018

<https://www.npr.org/sections/thetwo-

way/2017/06/22/533926978/census-finds-a-more-

diverse-america-as-whites-lag-growth>.

16) P. 29 "Minimum Wages in the United States by State

2019 | Statistic." *Statista*, Statista, Jan. 2019. 18 Dec.

2018 <www.statista.com/statistics/238997/minimum-

wage-by-us-state/.

17) P. 29 "Unemployment rates and earnings by educational

attainment." U.S. Bureau of Labor Statistics. U.S. Bureau

of Labor Statistics. 18 Dec. 2018

<https://www.bls.gov/emp/chart-unemployment-

earnings-education.htm>.

18) P. 30 See 3.

19) P. 30 Fontenot, Kayla, Jessica Semega, and Melissa Kollar.

"Income and Poverty in the United States: 2017." Income

and Poverty in the United States: 2017. 12 Sept. 2018. 18

Dec. 2018

<https://www.census.gov/library/publications/2018/de

mo/p60-263.html>.

20) P. 30 See 19.

21) P. 31 See 3.

A Pause for Clarity

22) P. 32 Partnership, Great Schools. "The Glossary of

Education Reform -." The Glossary of Education Reform.

2014. 6 Jan. 2019 <https://www.edglossary.org/>.

23) P. 32 See 22.

24) P. 33 See 22.

25) P. 33 US Department of Education, National Center for

Education Statistics. (2018). *Digest of Education

Statistics, 2016* (NCES 2017-094), Chapter 2. *And* "Class

of 2017 SAT Results – 2017 SAT Suite of Assessments

Program Results – The College Board." AP Program

Results: Class of 2016. 15 Mar. 2019. The College Board.

7 Jan. 2019

<https://reports.collegeboard.org/archive/sat-suite-

program-results/2017/class-2017-results>.

Chapter 2

26) P. 41 "Public School Revenue Sources." The Condition of

Education - Preprimary, Elementary, and Secondary

Education - Finances - Public School Revenue Sources -

Indicator April (2018). 2017. National Center for

Education Statistics. 5 Jan. 2019

<https://nces.ed.gov/programs/coe/indicator_cma.asp>.

27) P. 42 See 26.

28) P. 43 Strauss, Valerie. "Brown v. Board is 63 years old.

Was the Supreme Court's school desegregation ruling a

failure?" The Washington Post. 16 May 2017. WP

Company. 6 Jan. 2019

<https://www.washingtonpost.com/news/answer-

sheet/wp/2017/05/16/the-supreme-courts-historic-

brown-v-board-ruling-is-63-years-old-was-it-a-failure/>.

29) P. 44 Federal Housing Administration, *Underwriting*

Manual: Underwriting and Valuation Procedure Under

Title II of the National Housing Act With Revisions to April

1, 1936 (Washington, D.C.), Part II, Section 2, Rating of

Location.[1]

30) P. 44 See 29.

31) P. 44 See 29.

32) P. 45 See 29.

33) P. 46 Carr, James H. "The 1968 Fair Housing Act; 50 Years

Of Progress, Still An Uphill Climb To Equality." *Forbes*,

Forbes Magazine, 11 Apr. 2018. 9 Jan. 2019.

www.forbes.com/sites/jameshcarr/2018/04/11/the-

1968-fair-housing-act-50-years-of-progress-still-an-uphill-

climb-to-equality/#2992eabad328.

34) P. 47 See 33.

35) P. 47 Brown, Emma. "On the anniversary of Brown v. Board, new evidence that U.S. schools are resegregating." The Washington Post. 17 May 2016. WP Company. 4 Jan. 2019 <https://www.washingtonpost.com/news/education/wp/2016/05/17/on-the-anniversary-of-brown-v-board-new-evidence-that-u-s-schools-are-resegregating/?utm_term=.11d6b21c9e30>.

36) P. 48 Strauss, Valerie. "The reason America's schools are so segregated - and the only way to fix it." The Washington Post. 14 Dec. 2016. WP Company. 3 Jan. 2019 <https://www.washingtonpost.com/news/answer-sheet/wp/2016/12/14/the-reason-americas-schools-are-so-segregated-and-the-only-way-to-fix-it/?noredirect=on&utm_term=.6b402d455932>.

Chapter 3

37) P. 50 "The NCES Fast Facts Tool provides quick answers

to many education questions (National Center for

Education Statistics)." National Center for Education

Statistics (NCES) Home Page, a part of the U.S.

Department of Education. National Center for Education

Statistics. 2 Jan. 2019

<https://nces.ed.gov/fastfacts/display.asp?id=372>.

38) P. 50 See 37.

39) P. 51 Grawe, Nathan D. *Demographics and the Demand

for Higher Education*. Johns Hopkins University Press,

2018.

40) P. 51 See 39.

41) P. 51 See 39.

42) P. 51 See 39.

43) P. 54 "About Us." National Center for Education Statistics

- About Us. National Center for Education Statistics. 6

Jan. 2019 <https://nces.ed.gov/about/>.

44) P. 54 "Moody's: Small but notable rise expected in closures, mergers for smaller US colleges." Moodys.com. 25 Sept. 2015. Moody's Investors Service, Inc. 18 Dec. 2018 <https://www.moodys.com/research/Moodys-Small-but-notable-rise-expected-in-closures-mergers-for--PR_335314>.

45) P. 55 Shapiro, D., Dundar, A., Huie, F., Wakhungu, P.K., Bhimdiwali, A. & Wilson, S.E. (2018, December). Completing College: A National View of Student Completion Rates – Fall 2012 Cohort (Signature Report No. 16). Herndon, VA: National Student Clearinghouse Research Center.

46) P. 55 See 45.

47) P. 55 See 45.

48) P. 56 See 45.

49) P. 56 See 37.

50) P. 62 Compass, U.S. News College, et al. "The 10 Best Public Universities in America." *U.S. News & World*

Report, U.S. News & World Report, 2018,

www.usnews.com/best-colleges/rankings/national-

universities/top-public.

51) P. 68 Shapiro, D., Dundar, A., Huie, F., Wakhungu, P.K.,

Bhimdiwali, A., Nathan, A., & Youngsik, H. (2018, July).

Transfer and Mobility: A National View of Student

Movement in Postsecondary Institutions, Fall 2011

Cohort (Signature Report No. 15). Herndon, VA: National

Student Clearinghouse Research Center.

52) P. 69 Shapiro, D., Dundar, A., Wakhungu, P.K, Yuan, X., &

Harrell, A. (2015, July). *Transfer and Mobility: A National*

View of Student Movement in Postsecondary Institutions,

Fall 2008 Cohort (Signature Report No. 9). Herndon, VA:

National Student Clearinghouse Research Center.

53) P. 70 See 52.

Chapter 4

54) P. 99 Zillow, Inc. "Los Gatos CA Home Prices & Home

   Values." *Zillow*, 2018. 11, Oct. 2018.

   www.zillow.com/los-gatos-ca/home-values.

55) P. 99 Associated Press. "California Is Now the World's

   Fifth-Largest Economy, Surpassing United Kingdom." *Los*

   Angeles Times, Los Angeles Times, 4 May 2018,

   www.latimes.com/business/la-fi-california-economy-

   gdp-20180504-story.html.

56) P. 117 Clinedinst, Melissa, and Pooja Patel. *2018 State of*

   College Admission. National Association of College

   Admission Counseling, 2018, pp. 1–40, *2018 State of*

   College Admission.

57) P. 117 See 56.

Chapter 5

58) P.126 Susiepoppick. "Here's What the Average Grad

   Makes Right Out of College." *MONEY.com*, Money:

   Personal Finance News & Advice, 22 Apr. 2015. 20, Feb.

2019. <money.com/money/collection-post/3829776/heres-what-the-average-grad-makes-right-out-of-college/.

59) P.126 Shapiro, D., Dundar, A., Huie, F., Wakhungu, P., Yuan, X., Nathan, A & Bhimdiwala, A. (2018, February). Completing College: A State-Level View of Student Completion Rates (Signature Report No. 14a). Herndon, VA: National Student Clearinghouse Research Center.

60) P.128 "Starbucks®." *Starbucks Coffee Company*, Starbucks, 2018. Feb. 2019. <www.starbucks.com/careers/working-at-starbucks/education.

61) P.128 "Eligibility and Requirements | McDonald's." *Eligibility and Requirements | McDonald's*, McDonald's Corporation, 2018. Feb. 2019. <www.mcdonalds.com/us/en-us/community/hacer/eligibility_and_requirements.html.

62) P.128 "Target Scholarships." *College Scholarships.org.*,

College Scholarships.org., 2018. Feb. 2019.

<www.collegescholarships.org/scholarships/companies/t

arget.htm.

A Pause for Sanity

63) P.135 Hartocollis, Anemona. "He Took On the Voting

Rights Act and Won. Now He's Taking On Harvard." *The*

New York Times, The New York Times, 19 Nov. 2017. 24,

Jan. 2019.

www.nytimes.com/2017/11/19/us/affirmative-action-

lawsuits.html.

64) **P.136 See 63.**

65) P.140 Chua, Amy. *Battle Hymn of the Tiger Mother.*

Thorpe, 2012.

66) P.141 "UC Berkeley Fall Enrollment Data." *UC Berkeley*

Fall Enrollment Data | Office of Planning and Analysis,

University of California. Feb. 2019.

<opa.berkeley.edu/uc-berkeley-fall-enrollment-data.

67) P.141 "Quick Facts about UCLA." *Quick Facts - UCLA Undergraduate Admission*, University of California. Feb. 2019. <www.admission.ucla.edu/campusprofile.htm.

68) P. 141 "Undergraduate Student Profile." *Facts 2019*, Stanford University. Feb. 2019. <facts.stanford.edu/academics/undergraduate-profile.

69) P.141 "University of Southern California." *About USC*, University of Southern California. Feb. 2019. <about.usc.edu/facts.

70) P.141 "Student Profile." *Student Profile | Undergraduate Admissions*, University of Michigan. Feb. 2019. <admissions.umich.edu/apply/freshmen-applicants/student-profile.

71) P.141 "Admissions Statistics." *Harvard College*, Harvard College. Feb. 2019. <college.harvard.edu/admissions/admissions-statistics.